Improving Language Arts Instruction Through Research

Harold G. Shane
Professor of Education
and Dean
The School of Education
Indiana University

June Grant Mulry
Professor of Education
and Assistant Dean
The School of Education
Indiana University

ASSOCIATION FOR SUPERVISION AND CURRICULUM DEVELOPMENT, NEA
1201 Sixteenth Street, N. W., Washington 6, D. C.

Foreword

This report, *Improving Language Arts Instruction Through Research,* is based upon the needs that teachers themselves express in relation to instruction in the language arts, especially in the elementary school years. The co-authors, Harold G. Shane and June Grant Mulry, and their colleagues and assistants have conducted a comprehensive and thorough survey of research studies and reports in supplying the best available answers to the questions that teachers directed to them.

The statement they prepared is planned to afford direct assistance to teachers in relating research findings to the day-to-day problems of instruction in the various areas of the language arts. It is a practical document, yet one that offers a sound basis for curriculum planning and instruction.

This summary provides a valuable and ready reference to the research findings concerning the teaching of reading, writing, spelling, grammar, listening, foreign language, and speech for the period 1955-62.

April 1963
University of Florida
Gainesville, Florida

Kimball Wiles, *President, ASCD*
For the Executive Committee

Contents

Acknowledgments

At the annual meeting of the ASCD in 1953, the Publications Committee proposed that a pamphlet be devoted to a survey and interpretation of research in the language arts. *Research Helps in Teaching the Language Arts,* a 1955 publication of the Association, was issued.

Because of the success of this report, the Publications Committee recommended a second similar booklet. *Improving Language Arts Instruction Through Research* was then commissioned by the Executive Committee. Extensive work was begun on the compilation of new data. Approximately 1,600 articles and research reports published between 1955 and early 1962 were reviewed. About 800 of these writings were preserved in the form of research briefs and used in the preparation of *Improving Language Arts Instruction Through Research.*

Particular thanks are due to Donald Glendenning for his leadership and effort in directing the team of persons who located, carded, studied, and prepared the hundreds of research digests cited in the chapters that follow. Appreciation also is due Mary Tagge, Richard Williams, Dale Robey, and the more than 100 graduate students at Northwestern University and Indiana University whose work materially assisted the authors.

The interest and help of Ruth Strickland and certain students in her advanced graduate classes merit a warm expression of thanks. Many members of the National Council for Research in English, too, were helpful and generous with their time. A number of recent articles and reprints provided by NCRE members, not yet included in published lists of references, would have been omitted if Council members had not responded to a request for assistance. In addition, the writers wish to acknowledge the general advice and assistance they received from faculty members and librarians at Indiana University.

April 1963
Bloomington, Indiana

HAROLD G. SHANE
JUNE GRANT MULRY

From the Association

The Association acknowledges, with sincere appreciation, the courtesy of the many authors and publishers who have given permission for quotation or adaptation of materials in this volume. These original sources are keyed into the text and are given in full in the chapter bibliographies.

Lillian C. Paukner, Director, Division of Curriculum and Instruction, Upper Grade Department, Milwaukee Public Schools, Milwaukee, Wisconsin, represented the ASCD Executive Committee as reader of this booklet.

Final editing of the manuscript and the guiding of it through publication were the responsibility of Robert R. Leeper, Associate Secretary and Editor, ASCD Publications. Margaret Gill, Executive Secretary of ASCD, read the publication and gave valuable editorial advice. Permissions to quote were secured by Ruth P. Ely, ASCD Editorial Associate. Technical production of the volume was by Barbara Dickinson, Editorial Assistant, NEA Publications Division.

Chapter One

Research in the Language Arts

D ESPITE its relatively short history, modern research has proved its great value to mankind. As Walter Lippmann pointed out [1] over 30 years ago, perhaps mankind's greatest intellectual achievement has been the development of a system of inventing inventions—of deliberately questing for changes and improvements—through the scientific method of problem solving based on study and experimentation.

In the tradition of such pioneers in experimental science as Lister, Koch, and Pasteur, research has been carried forward in the language arts since the late 1800s. At present, in the 1960s, professional education is heir to vast stockpiles of research data that are promising means of improving practices in our schools from the nursery level through the graduate level.

The importance of language arts research. The research studies that have been completed in recent years are vitally important for several reasons. They offer clues as to ways we can improve practice, they suggest ways in which instructional and curricular issues can be resolved, and they supply the body of tested knowledge that helps bring professional status to the classroom teacher who has a grasp of it.

In fine, sound language arts research findings provide a basis for much of our long-range progress in improving the skills. Man very much needs to refine these skills in a world beset by problems in communication and human understanding.

Research as a threat. Although few of us may think of it in such terms, genuinely valuable research is a "threatening" thing. *Much of its importance resides in the extent to which it threatens our complacency, untested assumptions, and unexamined practices.* This point requires a few words of clarification.

Education, like other fields of endeavor, is influenced in some measure by custom, habit, tradition, and the sometimes *un*validated (although not

---

[1] In: *A Preface to Morals.* New York: The Macmillan Company, 1929.

necessarily *in*valid) statements made by authorities and national figures. Exciting, significant research is a constant threat to the accepted-but-un-examined—a threat to custom and tradition mirrored in educational practice. To make a contribution, research must either *confirm* the established but unsubstantiated or *threaten* and *upset* the status quo.

This monograph was prepared in an effort to summarize for persons working with children and youth some of the research findings in the language arts that have appeared since 1955, when the ASCD published its first review of such studies in the booklet, *Research Helps in Teaching the Language Arts.* The material in the chapters that follow is not a revision but an extension of and supplement to the language arts research published prior to 1955.

We hope that the trends, ideas, and conclusions assembled within these pages will in some respects be a "threat" to what teachers and administrators have been doing or how they have been educating in the classroom. We also hope that, in other respects, they will help to establish more firmly those instructional practices to which study and experiment have given added promise or validity.

How this booklet was prepared. Because *Improving Language Arts Instruction Through Research,* as previously noted, is designed to supplement and to complement the ASCD's 1955 language arts research booklet, a number of basic features in the *structure* of the earlier publication have been borrowed or adapted in the 1963 version. The present material was prepared as follows:

1. Research studies were selected in view of what *teachers themselves* said they wanted to know about issues and problems in language arts instruction. A nationwide sample of 387 classroom teachers, in 1959-60, studied the questions originally obtained from teachers in 1954-55, prior to the preparation of the original ASCD pamphlet. These 387 teachers then suggested the problems and questions for which answers based on research were to be sought in preparing *Improving Language Arts Instruction Through Research.* Their problem-questions are the ones on which the following chapters are focused.

2. Data from studies germane to the teachers' questions were compiled in ten categories: reading, handwriting, creative writing, spelling, language usage, children's literature, listening, mass media, foreign language, and oral English.

3. The data were extracted from research and writings that appeared between 1955 and the spring of 1962. More than 1,600 articles and reports were located in reference sources and preserved on bibliography cards. From among the 1,600-odd references, 844 entries proved to be of sufficient

promise and relevance to be studied in detail and abridged in the form of two-to-five-page research briefs.

4. The research briefs were classified in terms of the ten categories used in organizing the chapters in this monograph—reading, handwriting, and so on. Further screening of the research summaries resulted in the sections and subsections in each chapter.

Many teachers and most specialists in the language arts will note that the research and other publications cited, while reasonably numerous, are nonetheless far from being comprehensive. There are at least three explanations of those oversights and omissions that may be noted. First, selections were governed by information that teachers themselves said would be helpful to them in improving their teaching. Second, no research review *can* be comprehensive. Human judgment is fallible with respect to both the location and selection of significant language arts publications, especially in view of the large quantity published each year and the varied sources in which they appear. Third, limitation as to space in a pamphlet or monograph was a restrictive factor.

Chapter Two

The Realm of Reading

THE FIELD of reading continues to be the component of the language arts in which interest is both incandescent and widespread. This statement is supported by the distribution of research and general writings that have appeared since 1955.

Teachers' Questions Related to the Teaching of Reading

Teachers polled prior to the compilation of this research summary raised questions that fell into ten categories. These were:

1. What general trends and viewpoints are influencing practices in reading instruction?

2. What do parents and other persons not directly concerned with education say and how do they feel about the teaching of reading? (This query appears to reflect the "Great Debates" and "Great Reappraisals" with respect to public education that enlivened the years between 1950 and the present.)

3. What general reviews digest research data for teachers who have neither the time nor the library resources that are needed in order to study original sources?

4. What are current developments with respect to readiness as it pertains to reading?

5. What have research findings added to our knowledge of the role of phonetics in teaching reading, particularly during the primary school years?

6. What data have been accumulated with regard to methods of reading instruction?

7. What work is being done in vocabulary development?

8. What research has appeared with respect to reading ability and listening skills?

9. What developments in research provide us with new findings, germane to reading, in physiology—including the question of sex differences in readers?

10. What miscellaneous or "general interest" research in reading has appeared in recent years?

The ten clusters of questions related to reading that were raised by classroom teachers are themselves of some interest because of similarities and differences between the present list and the roster of questions obtained from classroom teachers in 1953-54, prior to preparation of the first ASCD language arts research review.[1] Interest remains keen with respect to methods of instruction and readiness, but less concern was expressed with regard to the use of commercial materials versus teacher-made materials and the evaluation of pupil progress. Queries with respect to public attitudes probably reflect a decade that bristled with such publications as Rudolf Flesch's *Why Johnny Can't Read* (52) or C. E. Walcutt's *Tomorrow's Illiterates* (199). Also, a greater interest in the physiology of the reader suggests the trend toward respect for and interest in disciplines with a bearing on education.

Organization of Chapter Two. The present chapter is built around the ten question-clusters listed here, each of which is considered in turn. The numbers in parentheses are keyed to coincide with the numbered and alphabetized references that appear at the close of Chapter Two.

General Trends and Viewpoints

Familiar names of established stature were associated with statements anent the general field of reading between 1955 and 1962. While new names, too, appeared, it seems a fitting tribute to the long-standing record of contributions from major figures to include in this introductory overview material from the late William S. Gray, from Ruth Strickland, Arthur I. Gates, David H. Russell, and Helen M. Robinson.

The broad overview. Shortly before his untimely, accidental death, Gray (71) placed on record his mellow retrospective wisdom with regard to a world view of current reading problems. The six problems he identified in an international context were (a) attaining functional literacy among adults, (b) providing improved instruction for children, (c) determining even more effective methods of teaching reading, (d) providing better materials, (e) developing further the ability to interpret and apply what is read, and (f) providing help for retarded readers. Gray's four points regarding the improvement of reading (71:17) are more pertinent to the improvement of instruction than his six general points, since they reflect a view based upon the years of highly influential research which he undertook at the University of Chicago:

[1] Cf. *Research Helps in Teaching the Language Arts.* Washington, D. C.: Association for Supervision and Curriculum Development, 1955. p. 4.

1. The same method does not secure equally satisfactory results in all schools and classrooms. This indicates that other factors, such as the teacher, the pupils, and the materials used, exert a vital influence on progress in learning to read.

2. Contrasting methods emphasize different aspects of reading. A phonic method gives most emphasis initially to word recognition. A word method gives most emphasis from the beginning to the meaning of what is read.

3. Contrasting methods start pupils toward maturity in reading over different routes. Sooner or later any specialized method must be supplemented to insure growth in all essential aspects of reading.

4. Best results are secured when both meaning and word-recognition skills are emphasized from the beginning.

Strickland (182) has added to the "general viewpoint" literature her thoughts as to what constitutes a challenging classroom milieu for reading. Her advice includes the admonition that the teacher remember that the individual child is engaged in the constant process of building the "self"; that nonstatic classroom environments should stimulate curiosity and encourage exploration, thinking, and problem solving; and that techniques in the use of resource material for independent learning need to be taught. A resourceful teacher, she points out, is the most important single element for stimulating children's growth and maturation. Two pertinent statements from Strickland's long article are all that space permits:

A large part of the task of creating a challenging environment for a child is concerned with studying him—his ways of thinking and responding and his interests and needs (182:75).

A challenging environment is in part physical and material, to be sure, but it is mainly psychological and inspirational; it is the social, emotional, and intellectual challenge that counts and everything in the environment is built to that end (182:77).

In broad strokes, Robinson (143) recently dealt more specifically with the topic of developing reading skills, concerning herself particularly with readiness, word recognition, meaning, rate, and interest. Representative of her points was the following:

It is clear, then, that we cannot wait for years of living to bring readiness for beginning reading. Instead, good teachers hasten children's progress in all aspects of readiness through well-planned programs to meet the specific needs of large and small groups and of individuals within each group (143:270).

Gates (59), within the past year, expressed himself with regard to controversies about teaching reading and suggested what he deemed the most promising ways to improve reading instruction. These included making efforts:

1. To increase the quantity and quality of "programmed" material for developing word recognition skill and the many specialized and subtle types of reading abilities needed at all educational levels

2. To find ways of making more effective use of such mechanical aids as motion and sound-motion pictures, television, and new types of "teaching machines" and other electronic devices

3. To provide means of increasing the insight and skill of teachers

4. To make available more time for individualized instruction.

He also noted that it is important to organize overall programs in which each procedure is effectively coordinated with the others so as to avoid "a hodgepodge of competitive devices."

Other current and readable general materials from Gates are his "The Teaching of Reading: Objective Evidence Versus Opinion" (64), material on helping the less able reader (66), and his painstaking reviews of Walcutt's *Tomorrow's Illiterates* and Trace's *What Ivan Knows That Johnny Doesn't* (57).

An article by Russell serves well as a final example of general comments on reading that merit attention. In "Personal Values in Reading" (151), he emphasized that reading is responding, identified three levels of response (151:3), and noted that ". . . most children will read at the surface level habitually unless the teacher encourages occasional penetration into new territory" (151:6).

Studies of Parental Opinion with Respect to Reading

Although rather few in number, several studies have been made of parents' opinions, and at least one dealt with children's views.

Parental views and pupil performance studies. Presnall's (132) inquiry led him to conclude that parents were greatly interested in the teaching of reading, although only 14 percent in a sample of 218 (a 60 percent response) felt that their children read poorly. His data suggested that the mothers and fathers in his sample wished more emphasis placed on phonics, more ability grouping in reading, and early memorization of the alphabet. Somewhat paradoxically, while 81 percent of the parents felt that their children read in a satisfactory manner, 60 percent believed that the methods to which they had been exposed in the grades were as good as or better than current methods.

Employing a team of trained interviewers, Larrick (98) set herself the task of ascertaining the interests, questions, and perhaps the anxieties that parents have about their children's reading. Only 8.3 percent of the random sample of 107 parents felt that their children were making poor progress. Larrick, with respect to the total study, concluded that the responses

". . . seem to indicate a general satisfaction with the progress that children are making in reading, some interest in how reading is taught, but greater interest in the development of reading pleasures, and a wide range of attitudes regarding the methods of teaching reading" (98:97).

The fact that parents evidently need not be alarmed about the quality of instruction has been borne out by findings of several researchers of which the Miller and Lanton (108) report is representative. In comparing "Reading Achievement of Children—Then and Now," Miller and Lanton learned that (after a 20-year interval and under carefully controlled conditions) elementary school children in the 'fifties were performing significantly better in reading on the tests used in the 'thirties. For example, in the 1950s the third, fifth, and eighth grade children tested scored six months above a comparable group from the 1930s in reading comprehension. Vocabularly scores were eight months ahead of those of their 1930 predecessors. A general review of a large number of comparison-of-achievement studies was published by Shane (161:263 ff.), which further substantiated the steady improvement made in children's academic progress in recent decades.

The child looks at reading. Reading from the viewpoint of the child was examined by Edwards (47) who worked with 66 retarded readers. Interview, observation, and "three-question" techniques were employed. The children's attitudes, with respect to their concept of what "good reading" was, were generally consistent. Among the findings were the points that children were greatly motivated by a quest for social acceptance by peers, parents, and teachers and that they identified good reading with speed and fluency.

Reviews of Research in Reading

Pursuant to the requests teachers voiced for a digest of research summaries in reading, a small sample of available materials is presented.

Research summaries. Russell (155), in 1958, summarized some 70 studies which he judged to have had a particular impact on reading. In 1961 he again selected and discussed "Reading Research That Makes a Difference" (154). These data covered a ten-year span and mirrored an expert's opinion on what have been significant contributions during a critical decade in United States education.

In 1961 Staiger (176) produced a 312-item bibliography of language arts studies that appeared during the preceding year. In addition to such conventional topics as reading or spelling, he includes "programs and curricula," "linguistics," "mass communication," "bilingualism," "folklore," and similar specialized research foci. The Staiger listings are not annotated. Strom (186), on the other hand, has prepared a smaller list restricted to secondary education that provides a helpful commentary. She reviewed and annotated a total of 84 studies that appeared during 1959 and 1960.

Representative of the more specialized research pieces is Robinson's (144) review of publications that dealt with factors which influence success in reading. Such writers as Goins, Orear, Sheldon and Carrillo, Davis, and Henry are cited.

The crystal ball. Some publications use a "crystal ball" approach to *suggest* rather than to *review* research.

Gates (61), for instance, in 1962 discussed recent trends and controversies that have implications for what *might* be done rather than what *has* been done in terms of research in reading.

Again, a subcommittee of the National Conference on Research in Reading under the chairmanship of Russell Stauffer (116) has prepared the manifesto, "Needed Research in Reading." This consists of 89 proposals or suggestions that are grouped under the ten headings which follow:

Beginning reading	Reading disability
Reading skills	Parents
Affective learning	School organization
Teacher education	Measurement, evaluation
Nature of reading process	Materials.

It should be understood that each of these headings was expanded explicitly with regard to *reading* by the Stauffer NCRE subcommittee.

Reading Readiness

In the 1955 ASCD monograph, *Research Helps in Teaching the Language Arts,* considerable attention was given to research that was relevant to readiness. Before turning to more recent data, it seems desirable to mention, in capsule form, the gist of the earlier review.

A retrospective glance. The 1955 monograph, citing 20-odd sources, pointed out that:

1. Readiness is a conception or perception that applies to the total learning experience, not reading *per se.*

2. Readiness, within limits, can be ascertained.

3. Mental age and I.Q. scores are indicative, to some degree, of readiness for reading, although opinions vary as to which and how many mental tests are valid indices.

4. Neither chronological age nor kindergarten teachers' subjective opinions were suitable bases for judging readiness.

5. Formal reading experiences should be postponed until an **M.A.** of 6 years and 6 months had been attained.

6. Many intangibles affect readiness and no *single* measure, judgment, or device can, at present, adequately determine it.[2]

In the past few years, then, what has been added to or subtracted from our fund of information bearing on reading readiness? Sources cited deliberately were selected to add to rather than duplicate the material in the 1955 ASCD report.

Recent research with implications for readiness. In terms of physical growth, one researcher, Karlin (90), has concluded that there is a distinct positive relationship between skeletal development and reading readiness. He worked with 111 first grade pupils from four public schools in the suburban New York area in order to discover what correlations if any might be found, respectively, among skeletal growth, height, and weight on the one hand and reading readiness scores and reading achievement test scores on the other. His findings included the point that "The relationship between skeletal development and reading scores is definite and may be considered a factor in reading-readiness."

In another journal article, Karlin (91) also reported his efforts to predict the probable success of a child in reading from readiness test scores on a nationally known test. The results obtained from his sample of six-year-olds led him to conclude that "It is virtually impossible to predict from the reading readiness test score how well any child in the sample will do on the reading test" (91:322). In other words, in this instance, the Metropolitan Readiness Test, Form R, failed to predict probable outcomes with respect to subsequent achievement. This result, Karlin pointed out, does not preclude the use of the test for diagnosis of possible language difficulties and problems in visual perception.

Matched groups of kindergarten children in the vicinity of St. Louis were recruited by Blakely and Shadle (13) for participation in a 1961 study intended to compare the effect of a basal reader and an experience-centered program on reading readiness. The same teacher worked with both groups in an effort to reduce the vagaries of personality and instruction. Although the modest size of the sample—28 boys and 28 girls—made sweeping generalizations a bit hazardous, the findings were of interest:

1. The experimental (i.e., experience-centered) group made more statistically significant gains on the Reading Readiness Appraisal Check and on the Maturity Check than did the basal reader group. The experimental group also outscored the basal group on the Scott-Foresman end-of-the-book test, although not to a significant degree.

[2] For more comprehensive information, cf. *Research Helps in Teaching the Language Arts,* p. 5 ff.

2. Kindergarten boys in particular made significantly better progress than girls in the experience-activity approach to reading, a finding that prompted the recommendation that young males be more widely exposed to experiences than to workbooks at the 5-year-old level.

Helpful and practical proposals as to how the teacher can make use of experiences that motivate children were listed by Crosby (40). She also presented a substantial statement of criteria which can be used in determining whether or not a child is reading with meaning.

Petty (126) also made a useful contribution with a bearing on readiness in an article treating critical reading at the primary level. One of his points was that the potential ability to engage in critical thinking should be cultivated before actual reading is done because of its relationship to critical thinking—and that the readiness stage should focus on this end.

A résumé of one more study—a longitudinal one—should suffice to round out the present digest of current readiness data. Bradley (24) undertook to clarify the value of a thorough stress on readiness in all school learnings, including reading. Two groups of 31 first grade children were matched on four counts: sex, chronological age, I.Q., and socioeconomic status. Their teachers, too, were paired with respect to such characteristics as ratings, experience, preparation, and grades previously taught. The "experimental" group was given no systematic reading instruction until each child was deemed "ready," while the control group was instructed as the school's teaching guides directed.

Results, similar to those reported in a number of comparable studies, both recent and vintage ones, were as follows:

1. Testing indicated that the experimental group read as well as the control group at the end of grade two.

2. Achievement was comparable at the end of three years with a slight advantage displayed in work-study and basic language skills by the experimental group.

Bradley noted (24:265) that "The early intensive start in reading and other academic subjects did not result in greater gains for the control group." Presumably, it did them no harm either. Bradley also made the point that the experimental group had more varied experiences than the formally instructed group. This leaves unanswered the question of why their gains were not more spectacular if an emphasis on readiness experiences is more valuable than traditional approaches to learning.

On the whole, in reviewing material related to reading readiness, one is impressed by the way in which a myriad of studies have added to our present fund of professional knowledge. The picture with respect to readiness is like a mosaic, built bit by bit into an increasingly clear total pattern. At the same time, one is somewhat frustrated at how much yet needs to be known!

It was, alas, over 26 years ago when Gates and Bond (67) remarked that "It appears that readiness for reading is something to *develop* rather than something merely to *wait* for." We are still in pursuit of a sufficient quantity of definitive information that shows how we can best develop readiness.

Phonics: Durable Object of Research

The role of phonics [3] continues to be a prime conversation piece in the teaching of reading, the subject of considerable research, and the source of vigorous opinion that is often quite unrelated to research!

The status of research in phonics. The generally inconclusive nature of much of the current literature was revealed in a 1958 doctoral study made by Morrone (113) at the University of Pittsburgh. He reviewed 198 references of which 101 were original. Sad to relate, his findings suggested that "The scientific investigations of phonics in reading and spelling do not reveal much unrefutable evidence." He also stated that "Disagreement exists as to the approach and amount of phonic instruction teachers should utilize in reading; however, most of the scientifically accurate experiments show that phonics have considerable value to the learner in the reading process."

Nila B. Smith (169) also has gone on record with certain generalizations about phonics. Among her points are these:

1. It cannot be assumed that *all* children need phonics.

2. Phonics is effective with children who need word-recognition help, but its greatest effectiveness is attained when it is taught functionally and is related to children's reading needs.

3. It is advisable to delay intensive phonics instruction until a child has attained a mental age of seven years.[4]

4. Phonics instruction is most valuable at the second- and third-grade levels.

5. The use of configuration clues and context clues should be supplemented with phonics.

[3] Some confusion surrounds the use of the term *phonics*. This plural noun, which is construed as singular, refers to the science of sounds and also to the use of *phonetics* in teaching reading. *Phonetics* (also a plural noun construed as singular) refers to those aspects of language study that are concerned with speech sounds and with the way the sounds are represented in written form. Cognate terms with which teachers may wish to be familiar include *phonogram,* a sign or symbol that represents sounds. syllables, or words, and *phoneme* which refers to a family of related speech sounds represented by the same written symbol: e.g., the *s* sound in *s*ing, *s*ound, or *s*ad.

[4] Morrone, cited earlier, apparently would not agree. "There is little available evidence," he stated, "that discloses the optimum mental age to teach phonics."

14

6. It would be well to give more attention to both visual and auditory discrimination in teaching all types of word recognition.

What does research say about phonics? A rather important question, in view of long and heated discussion, is "What *can* be said about phonics as a tool in instruction?" Actually, any specific generalization seems perilous, but a few current researchers are cited here in terms of which the reader may make his choices and place his bets!

Clymer (35) used four popular sets of readers to ascertain what phonic generalizations were taught in the primary grades. Forty-four such generalizations were identified. Also, a list of 2,200 words was compiled to determine how many of the 2,200 words actually conformed to the generalizations. Only nine words conformed to the 44 generalizations, and but 22 conformed to three-quarters of the generalizations—a finding that suggests that English is not an especially consistent language with respect to pronunciation of primary level words.

In an interesting, protracted piece of research, Sparks and Fay (172) set themselves the task of determining how the Phonetic Keys to Reading method compared with a conventional basic reading program. Carried on over a four-year period with 824 pupils in two Kentucky schools, this longitudinal study led Sparks and Fay to the conclusion that the "Phonetic Keys" method initially led to superior [5] results with respect to reading vocabulary and comprehension at the end of grade two and that the children appeared to do better in connection with such activities as following directions. However, at the end of grade four there was no significant difference between the two groups of 418 and 406 children in reading comprehension, vocabulary, or speed. Also, the basic program group was apparently superior in reading accurately. The researchers concluded that "Since no advantage was found in using *Phonetic Keys to Reading* as a basal reading program, the common practice of using the *Phonetic Keys to Reading* for a separate phonics period or to supplement another basal reading series should be seriously questioned" (172:390). Conversely, the use of the "Phonetic Keys" presumably produced no iniquitous results!

Templin (187), working in Minneapolis with fourth graders, delved into phonic knowledge and the matter of its relationship to spelling and reading achievement. Among her findings were the following:

1. The correlations between phonic knowledge and spelling are somewhat higher than between phonic knowledge and reading.

2. The better spellers as compared to the poorer spellers received the higher scores on all tests except the sound discrimination test.

---

[5] The researchers note that the "superiority" may have been spurious because of the tests used.

3. The comparison of the deviate reading groups indicates the better readers received the higher scores on all tests.

4. The phonic knowledge scores are noted to be significantly higher when a recognition rather than a recall technique of measurement is used.

5. Among the recognition measures, significantly higher scores are obtained when the stimulus is a familiar word rather than a sound or a nonsense-word.

Rudisill (149), in a somewhat comparable study of interrelations of functional phonic knowledge, reading, spelling, and mental age found (a) common factors among reading, spelling, and phonic knowledge independent of intelligence; (b) higher correlations than those obtained in other studies in which ability to produce or recognize sounds of individual letters or letter combinations was the measure of phonic ability; and (c) that the ability to identify sounds in normal word pronunciation and to relate these sounds to letter symbols encompasses the major contribution of phonics to reading and spelling achievement.

The Mulder and Curtin (114) inquiry, which utilized tape recorders [6] with 63 Oregon youngsters, was designed to determine whether or not ". . . a relationship exists between (a) the ability to fuse phonetic elements, presented orally, into words and (b) the ability to read" (114:121). Their study indicated that a positive relation did exist, in the fourth grade studied, between silent reading ability and the ability to synthesize phonetic elements of words presented orally. Furthermore, good readers possessed the ability to synthesize phonetic elements into words to a marked degree, while poor readers were deficient in the ability to synthesize phonic elements of words into meaningful word patterns.

A useful historical study was made by Massey (107), who reviewed literature pertaining to approaches to word perception between 1607 and 1955. His data justified these conclusions:

1. The yearbooks of the National Society for the Study of Education since 1925 have consistently recommended a balanced program of word-perception based on results of research.

2. Historically the answer to the question as to the method to be employed in developing word-perception has been sought in synthetic and analytic approaches.

3. A single approach to word-perception, such as the alphabet, phonic, or word method has led to a program which was lacking in the development of some of the needed word-attack skills, abilities, and understandings necessary for independence in reading.

---

[6] Mulder and Curtin, for purposes of uniformity in presentation, made a tape of 78 one-syllable nouns for their vocal phonics test. Speakers on the tape pronounced the words for groups of about 20 pupils, utilizing each of the phonetic elements. Pupils checked answer sheets which contained three pictures for each test item.

4. On the basis of historical evidence, there would appear to be little justification for a return to a single approach to word-perception, such as the alphabet-phonetic approach currently being advocated.

A study of 14 first grade groups made by Bear (7) may be cited as an example of recent reports dealing with diverse methods involving the use of phonics. His results supported the synthetic method as distinct from the analytic or whole-word method.

Although the furore surrounding Rudolf Flesch's 1955 book, *Why Johnny Can't Read* (52), had abated during most of the period covered by this monograph, some articles that dealt with his views regarding phonics appeared. Representative of writings that were designed to show that his data were ineptly handled is Carroll's (29) analysis.

Writings by two English proponents of phonics, J. C. Daniels and H. Diack (43), were the objects of critical, although not scathing, comment from Russell (153) and a heated rejoinder from Gates (60). The latter, with reference to Diack's *Reading and the Psychology of Perception* (44), stated that the experimental and logical evidence presented in Diack's book does not justify his conviction that phonics alone can teach reading (60:527-28).

How-To-Do-It Research Related to Methods of Teaching Reading

During the past six or eight years, two topics associated with reading methods have assumed increased importance if available literature is any index. As many readers would guess, these are (a) individualized reading (including grouping) and (b) the use of the self-instructional devices familiarly known as teaching machines. In addition to these two topics, other long-standing objects of research about which teachers requested information are mentioned in the following pages: studies of fast- and slow-achieving readers; reading and intelligence; interest and purpose as these relate to reading; inquiries pertaining to perception, speed, comprehension, and critical reading; and miscellaneous investigations including a few studies carried out with adults.

Individualized methods in reading instruction. As might be inferred because of the popularity of so-called individualized procedures or practices in the teaching of reading, most of the research and literature is favorable in tone. For an example of recent generally favorable commentaries, the reader is referred to Witty (206), who has prepared a summary and evaluation of individualized methods.

A critique of the Witty article made by Veatch (196) lends added interest to his remarks. She contended that Witty ". . . does not make clear the difference between the individualized, self-selection approach and the ability-grouped, basal reader approach. . . ." She also stated that she was ". . . appalled at the finality with which Dr. Witty and other able, well-known people have pre-judged or incorrectly judged this development as (a) unimportant, or (b) a 'fad,' or (c) something good teachers have always done." The Witty and Veatch statements, both of which appeared in *Elementary English,* provide a lively introduction to the topic.

Peripherally related to individualized reading are articles by Gates (58) and Mills (110). Respectively, they concerned themselves with the age for teaching beginning reading and with word recognition—both relevant to individualization. Mills' purpose was to determine the teaching method or combination of methods most effective in teaching word recognition to various types of individual children. Four methods explored were the visual, phonic, kinesthetic, and a combination of all three. Insofar as his sample of 58 young Floridians in grades two to four were concerned, individual pupils learned to recognize words more efficiently by different methods, no one method being best for all.

With respect to subgroups in his relatively small sample, Mills made the following observations:

1. *Children of low intelligence.* The phonic method is least effective for this group. The kinesthetic method is best in the greatest number of cases, but it is not statistically better than the visual and the combination methods.

2. *Children of average intelligence.* For the majority of cases in this group the kinesthetic method is the least effective. The phonic method showed no statistical significance in either direction. The combination and the visual methods seemed to be about the same for this group.

3. *Children of high intelligence.* In this group conclusions were not given because all children tended to learn words readily regardless of the teaching method used. However, the visual method *did prove* superior to the kinesthetic method for this group.

4. *Seven-year-olds.* The visual method seemed to be best and the poorest was the kinesthetic method.

5. *Eight-year-olds.* The best method for this group was the kinesthetic method; significantly better than the phonic and somewhat better than the other two methods.

6. *Nine-year-olds.* The visual method seemed to be better than the kinesthetic method but no one of the four was outstandingly effective.

In closing his report, Mills (110:225) wrote that "In general, the higher the intelligence, the more readily children learn words. However, there is no consistent relation between age and a child's readiness to learn words for the three age groups studied." Furthermore, "This research indicates the need for the concentration of energies on finding out *which* method is best for *which* children rather than developing a recipe or 'a best method' that will serve for all children all the time." Proponents of individualization, take notice!

The rather obvious but nonetheless important research study comparing "individualized" and "basal reader" approaches to the teaching of reading flowered—or perhaps exploded is a better term—during the late 1950s and early 1960s. From Alachua County, Florida, in the East to San Diego County, California, in the West, the reports came in! Studies by Allen (195), Clark and Gordon (33), Bohnhorst and Sellars (20), and Groff (78) are representative of data now in print.

Allen's San Diego County study, a three-year one, investigated three approaches identified as (a) basal, (b) individualized, and (c) language-experience. The Clark and Gordon project, employing two second grades in Florida, compared an experimental (individualized) group and a control (basal reading series) group. Among the findings:

1. A significant gain was made by the experimental group over the control group. "In the semester's time, less than four months, the control group gained an average of 3.04 months; the experimental group gained 7.32 months."

2. An increase was also noted in the spread in achievement. "The control group range stayed at a two-grade, nine months spread, while the individualized reading group went from a two-grade, two months range to one of three-grade, two months."

3. The individualized reading program using limited resources in this particular study was "demonstrably superior to the standard reading program."

Bohnhorst and Sellars, from their Atlanta study, inferred that individualized work was especially effective with the most able readers. Groff's article offered a number of suggestions that were valuable not only for individualized experiences but for general methods of teaching reading, too.

Grouping for instruction, a venerable means of providing for differences in human individuality, continued to capture the interest and draw forth the effort of research workers concerned with reading. Sartain (158) compared what he termed "individualized self-selection" and ability grouping at the second grade level. Since neither group significantly outperformed the other, he felt (in apparent contrast to the Clark-Gordon conclusions above) that ". . . there is no reason to forfeit the advantages of a well planned basal system."

Bremer (26), working in Amarillo, Texas, investigated first graders' achievement in two paired classes that had been grouped in terms of "high-readiness" and "low-readiness." Eight factors such as sex, class size, and family socioeconomic status were considered when the groups were matched. His findings suggested the importance of flexible groupings of readers.

Although their work was not "research" in the strict sense of the word, three fourth grade teachers—Aaron, Goodwin, and Kent (1)—reported with enthusiasm their design for cross-class grouping for reading instruction. They devised a modified team-teaching technique that took into account their pupils' varied interests, ability, and experience. Hart's (81) comparison of homogeneous versus heterogeneous grouping leads to the conclusion that his study ". . . gives strong support to those teachers and administrators who believe that ability grouping has merit and deserves serious consideration."

Two more examples serve to round out this abridgment of recent developments in individualized reading and grouping. Kingsley (94) endeavored to learn the outcomes of an individualized reading program based entirely on the use of library books. Her Bellingham, Washington, study was limited to sixth graders, covered one academic year, and was based on individually guided reading and conferences. Both children and teacher kept records for purposes of evaluation, and provision was made for individual oral reading sessions. Kingsley obtained gratifying increases in reading comprehension, a modest increase in speed, and little vocabulary improvement. Other results:

1. Students who were above grade level and students below grade level both averaged 9½ months growth.

2. Big individual gains were made in both the above- and below-average groups.

3. The "bulge" in grade score distribution moved up the scale.

4. Children read about fifty books per child, with a range from 13 to 103.

Warford (201) also reported on a "library approach" to reading improvement, using 80 high-interest level books to stimulate progress. Warford reported that the personal potential of pupils was more fully realized and their liking for good books more powerfully stimulated as a result of the program.

Since individualized reading, in some of its aspects, makes use of trade books, teachers doubtless will find much of interest in Russell's (150) recent (1961) analysis of a sample of easy-to-read books for primary children. His analysis was based on (a) content, attractiveness, and interest value; (b) vocabulary comparisons; (c) Spache Readability Formula ratings; and (d) comments obtained from groups of first and second graders and their teachers. Among Russell's evaluations were these:

1. The children's trade books are factual, fictional, and attractive (both the writing and the illustrations are attractive); "they vary widely in format, difficulty, and literary merit."

2. More children can read independently using these books, but children who are beginning to learn to read are not provided for.

20

3. Most easy-to-read books are equal in difficulty to first and second readers (level one) of two "well-known basal series."

4. Each provides reading material about equal to a second preprimer; these ten provide as much material as five basal readers. Each trade book is about three times as expensive as the first grade readers.

5. Reading difficulty varies from grade 1.7 to grade 2.9 according to the Spache Readability Formula.

6. Trade books are generally more attractive in format, although there is no evidence that this would make them more teachable.

7. Trade books seem to be suitable for "a few superior readers near the end of grade one, average or superior readers in grade two, and average and below average readers in the first half of the third grade."

8. Children's favorable reactions to the books "far outweigh their negative criticisms."

9. A shelf of good books in the classroom would stimulate interest in reading, but would not be adequate for the teaching of reading.

Patently, Russell's appraisals are useful ones for the teacher who is casting an eye on the library shelf prior to compiling a collection of titles that will be helpful in an individualized program.

Although not related directly to individualized reading, Betts' (10) discussion of "Reading and the Fourth R" is of interest. The fourth R refers to "regimentation," and this seasoned writer made the point—through examples—that averages must be used with caution in gauging reading achievement.

What do teaching machines teach? Much of the research that has been concerned with self-instructional devices, at least as it pertains to reading, is relatively recent and limited. This is true, that is, if one rules out such familiar machines as the tachistoscope or devices that govern or pace reading rates.

Gates (62), in a historical overview, treated "Teaching Machines in Perspective." His article provides useful background information and evaluations. Also helpful is Karlin's (89) view of research pertaining to machines and reading. On the basis of a dozen investigations which he summarized, Karlin noted that gains can be achieved through the use of mechanical devices but that "Outcomes in speed of reading similar to those achieved through the use of special instruments may be expected from suitable reading instruction which does not include these same instruments."

The controversial New Castle filmstrip method of teaching beginning reading continued to appear in print as late as 1960. Lichtenstein's (103) work tended to verify the lack of low primary-grade reading scores claimed in the original New Castle studies by McCracken.

Machine-centered versus book-centered instruction was the object of an adult-level inquiry carried out by Thompson (188). His subjects were 438 Air Force officers. The men involved were divided among a Machine Group, a Book Group, and a Control Group, the latter receiving no special instruction in reading. The Machine Group (58 words per minute gain) excelled the Book Group (50 w.p.m. gain) and the Control Group (40 w.p.m. gain) in *speed*. Changes in *comprehension* were very slight with no statistically significant differences noted at the 5 percent level. *"Flexibility"* (i.e., ". . . the ability to make an intelligent adjustment of reading speed to the difficulty of the reading material") suffered a slight loss in all three groups.

Because the great current interest in *newer* types of teaching machines is so recent, it may be two or three years before more definitive research data appear in print to help answer the question of what—and how well— programed learning can contribute to reading instruction. Insofar as standard long-established mechanical devices are concerned, their utility and limitations long have been known in our reading clinics and laboratories.

Working with readers of high and low achievement. Attention is now directed to research reports dealing with "able" and "slow" readers and to appraisals of clinical resources provided for them.

Of general interest was Geboe's (68) evaluation of the use of folklore as a means of stimulating and challenging 33 children of third grade age. Their responses indicated that myths were preferred by most of the able young readers, with fables and fairy tales lagging. Adult readers and tape recordings were favored as means of hearing a story—presumably filmstrip presentations of folklore were preferable to motion picture films, probably because the children liked the opportunity for discussion and questions which the filmstrips permitted.

Sister Josephina (164) surveyed and reported research pertaining to the reading ability of the gifted and concluded that ". . . the literature is marked by an absence of statistical treatment dealing with the problem."

Children with average reading scores two or more years in advance of mental age scores were studied by Raymond (136). The 50 boys she sampled in three Massachusetts school systems were examined to determine relationships between memory span and associative learning test findings of these high achievers. Memory span test results showed visual skills in excess of auditory skills and that the 50 lads remembered sentences better than words to a significant degree. With respect to associative learning test findings:

1. Reading achievers make significantly higher scores on associative tests with a visual-auditory presentation than with a visual-visual presentation.

2. Reading achievers make significantly higher scores on associative tests employing geometry-test targets than on those employing word-like targets.

3. Reading achievers make superior scores on tests employing visual, auditory, and voco-motor associations.

4. Reading achievers make mental age scores on an oral vocabulary test (antonyms) equivalent to their Binet mental age scores.

The tests used and other detailed information are given in Raymond's report.

A comparative study of the achievement of 50 children in grades one through seven was reported by Hoyt and Blackmore (86). Through the review of the children's cumulative records it was learned that ". . . reading achievement and capacity paralleled consistently for the first three or four grades, but at the fourth or fifth grades a minor deviation between actual achievement and expected achievement began to occur. This deviation continued throughout the grades up to seven, and about 85 percent of the cases did not return to their expected achievement levels."

Bliesmer (14) compared the results of various capacity tests used with retarded readers in a Texas city that was not identified. Among his conclusions were:

1. The Durrell-Sullivan test tends to give higher estimates of reading capacity than does the Stanford-Binet scale, while the Kuhlmann-Anderson and the California tests tend to give lower estimates.

2. Utilizing median values obtained in Kuhlmann-Anderson, Durrell-Sullivan, and California total scores does not appear to aid greatly in obtaining approximations of Stanford-Binet estimates.

3. None of the group tests used in this study yields estimates which might be considered adequate approximations of Stanford-Binet estimates.

The role of visual and kinesthetic factors in reading failure was probed in the University Elementary School of the University of California at Los Angeles through the use of 27 boys in an experimental group and 29 in a control group. Roberts and Coleman (140), the investigators, ascertained that reading failure cases were significantly inferior to normal readers on a test of visual perception. Also, as a group, reading failure cases were significantly less efficient than normal readers when learning new materials by means of visual cues only. Roberts and Coleman discovered that the group of reading failure cases were significantly better able to learn new materials by methods which included kinesthetic components than those which employed visual stimuli only, and as a group, normal readers were not significantly aided in learning new material by the addition of kinesthetic elements to visual ones. Finally, reading failure cases who achieved normal scores on the test of visual perception did not profit appreciably from the addition of kinesthetic to visual cues in learning, and normal readers who achieved lower than average scores on the test in visual perception did learn faster with the addition of kinesthetic visual cues.

The happy point that retarded readers can and do develop lasting reading habits characterized by wide interests and discriminating tastes was made by Robinson (142). Her comments, including useful suggestions for helping the slow reader, are of particular value to classroom teachers.

Kingston and Clay (95), in order to study reading and academic achievement, selected 274 males from Texas College of Agriculture and Mechanics who were majoring in business administration, agriculture, or engineering. It was the purpose of the study to determine the influence of a remedial reading course, taken at the freshman level, on the students' subsequent scholastic records. Participation in a college reading program apparently assists students, Kingston and Clay reported, ". . . when their curriculum is largely linguistic in nature." They also felt that reading training permanently influenced performance.

Several other follow-up studies have been made in recent years with respect to the value of clinical-remedial services. Such reports have been made by Johnson (88), Ranson (135), and Tufvander and Zintz (192). Clinics at Temple University, the University of Missouri, and Iowa State Teachers College, respectively, were involved. Johnson analyzed the cases of children in the Temple program to ascertain the nature of their difficulties. Ranson evaluated the effectiveness of the University of Missouri Reading and Study Skills Clinic, and the Tufvander-Zintz appraisal served the same purpose at the Iowa State Teachers College Educational Clinic. The findings were to the credit of the clinics and clearly substantiated their value in institutions of higher education and—by inference—in public school systems.

Reading and intelligence. Representative of research and writings related to reading and intelligence were publications by Barbe (6), Bond and Clymer (21), and Larson and Selland (99). Assuming that group I.Q. tests ". . . are actually little more than measures of reading ability," Barbe attempted to determine whether there would be an improvement in mental maturity test scores pursuant to a 12-week college reading program. Reading rates improved, but the mean I.Q. difference, however, was insignificant.

Bond and Clymer worked with 87 fourth graders to establish interrelationships among SRA Primary Mental Abilities Test, other mental characteristics, and reading abilities. In general, significant interrelationships were identified. The Larson-Selland study compared the mental and reading ages of 475 sixth graders. The median reading age for their group of North Dakota children was one month below the norm for the Iowa Basic Skills Test, Part I, despite the fact that the median I.Q. score (Kuhlmann-

Anderson) was 108. Also, 77 percent of the underachievers had I.Q. scores of 100 or above.

It would appear that research relating reading and intelligence continues to produce unpredictable results and that variables that are not—or cannot be—controlled continue to be of great importance in influencing both the I.Q. score and achievement in reading.

Interest and purpose. The way children *feel* about reading continued to intrigue researchers in recent years. Hogenson (85) studied two carefully matched groups of children, 50 in all, and learned that the experimental group (which had expressed a desire to improve in reading) excelled the control group. Comprehension, speed, and vocabulary were compared.

Through the use of two especially designed instruments, Bernstein (8) endeavored to identify relationships between interest and reading comprehension at the ninth grade level. One hundred children participated in reading "high interest" and "low interest" stories that were rewritten to equate both tales with respect to Flesch, Lorge, and Dale-Chall readability formulas. As might have been predicted, the high interest level story produced superior comprehension scores. The fact that a *modern* tale was used as a high interest item and that Hawthorne's *The House of the Seven Gables* was rewritten as the low interest piece may further have influenced the outcome.

Letson's (101) investigation of the influence of material and purpose on reading rate also is relevant here. He drew the inference that:

> The difficulty of the material exerts a greater influence on rate than does the purpose. Slowing down to read more difficult material is important to good comprehension, but it is not necessary to slow down for mastery of the material, provided the difficulty level of the material remains constant. The call to read for mastery appears to engender an alertness above normal, and such a mental set renders the reader capable of reading with greater comprehension and speed.

A review of writings and research that concerned itself with readers' predispositions as a factor influencing critical reading is available to students seeking detailed information. Eller and Dykstra (48) made this review, which includes the work of Crossen, Collier, Deutscher and Chein, and Berenda. According to Eller and Dykstra, the mechanics of reading are emphasized to the detriment of the more intellectual aspects such as critical reading.

Speed and comprehension; perception and critical reading. Additions to our fund of knowledge with respect to speed and comprehension have been made by several research workers. Cook (38) compared comprehension scores obtained before and after a time announcement. Working with slow and fast readers, respectively, he learned that the slow readers, but not the fast ones, were adversely influenced by time pressure. In other words, slower readers were more prone to become "rattled" and to comprehend less. Letson (102), with a sample of 601 college freshmen, reported along with other findings that the relationship between speed and comprehension is *high* when comprehension is identified with the the number of right responses and is *negative* ". . . when comprehension is the ratio of right responses and the number attempted" and that the difficulty of the material read adversely affects comprehension when one reads rapidly.

Cosper and Kephart (39) developed a remedial program for university students and learned that speed could be increased far more than comprehension and that 60 percent of the speed-rate gains were retained after 14 months. Case study methods used by Pickarz (127) with 26 sixth graders revealed high ability level readers were able to get more meaning from the printed page than did low level readers who gave only passing attention to implied meanings and to critical evaluation. This conclusion confirms what many teachers have suspected, namely, that good readers participate with more insight in the reading process than poor ones.

Working in Ohio, McCullough (105) studied 258 second grade and fourth grade youngsters to determine whether or not there is a common factor involved in different types of reading comprehension. She was led to believe that a relationship does exist among different types of comprehension (e.g., sequence, drawing conclusions), but that testing one kind of comprehension could not be relied on as an index to all types.

A useful survey of conclusions was reached through word perception studies completed by Russell and Groff (156). They investigated the level of competence in visual perception of 120 Chicago area first grade children and the correlation of their perceptual abilities with achievement in reading. Wide individual variations were noted, several types of perceptual ability were identified, and it was found that some children are part perceivers. Also, in the Goins inquiry (70), tachistoscopic training did not increase the reading ability of her unselected first grade groups.

Insofar as critical reading is concerned, Spencer and Russell (173) dealt with research on the reading of verbal problems for their 1960 National Council of Teachers of Mathematics Yearbook report on "Reading in Arithmetic." They list a large number of explicitly helpful suggestions for the teacher to consider in improving the critical reading of problems. For example, "Give specific help in building understanding of quantitative terms like *numerator* and *acre* and of processes such as obtaining a batting average. . ." and, "Without giving numbers, have children state how they would solve problems such as 'Tom is a boy who got three separate birthday gifts of money. He wants to know if he has enough money to buy a basketball. What should he do?' "

A general assessment of critical reading in the content areas made by Artley (5) contained a variety of useful suggestions. Williams' (202) investigation of provisions for critical reading in basic readers (preprimers through grade six) also contains points, seven in all, suggesting how teachers can promote growth in the ability to read critically.

Studies of reading involving adult populations. In addition to adult-level investigations involving reading, several general or miscellaneous publications merit more than perfunctory attention. An Air Force project undertaken by Stordahl and Christensen (181) indicated that study techniques such as underlining, outlining, or summarizing required *training* experiences to make them effective.

Standlee and Fattu (178) scrutinized eight Navy publications to determine readability and interest value. As veterans might guess, reading ease scores were well above the fourth grade "functional literacy" level, and the two "most interesting" of the eight Navy publications, as identified by enlisted men, were the two scored as easiest to read.

A rather recondite inquiry was made to determine, with a college population, whether improvement of vocabulary and reading comprehension could be predicted from scores on the ACE Language Test, the Brown-Holzmann "Survey of Study Habits and Attitudes" (SSHA), and from hysteria and psychasthenia (anxiety neurosis) scores on the MMPI. Chansky and Bregman (31), the investigators, found that their intercorrelations indicated ". . . that the pattern of scores which predispose a student to improvement in reading is: low psychasthenia, low verbal aptitude, that is, low in relation to the group, and good study habits." Ahmann and Glock (92) also have appraised (at the college level) the "Survey of Study Habits and Attitudes." It was their conclusion that this device was of little use in a freshman testing battery intended for use in connection with a reading improvement program.

Vocabulary Studies

The likelihood that mass media are influencing children's communication skills lends enhanced interest to recent vocabulary studies which reflect a decade or more of universalized televiewing in the United States. It seems appropriate at this point to mention the Dale-Reichert (42) *Bibliography of Vocabulary Studies* (revised) to those who seek detailed information on this topic. Carefully categorized, this publication is of enduring value and modestly priced.

Children's word knowledge. As a rule, vocabulary studies are monuments to patience. Among recent ventures is Repp's (139) tabulation and comparison of vocabularies used in five popular third grade arithmetic textbooks. She found marked eccentricities in vocabulary practices. For instance, 348 pages out of 1,645 introduced no new words, while four out of the five texts sometimes had 60 or more new, different words appearing on a single page. The reading comprehension problem here seems a self-evident challenge to both children and teachers.

Shibles (163) raised the question, "How many words does a first grade child know?" The conclusions drawn were from a Maine sample of 183 monolingual and bilingual children. Sample finding: the monolingual children, with a median I.Q. of 109.6, had a mean basic vocabulary of 18,924 words plus a derived vocabulary of 7,438 words. Eight of Shibles' conclusions follow:

1. First grade children apparently have a much larger vocabulary than has been previously estimated.

2. The utilization of an unabridged dictionary as a basis of word sampling has resulted in substantially greater understanding of vocabulary estimates over the abridged dictionary and word lists.

3. The size of the understood vocabulary of first grade children appears to have a fairly steady growth with measured intelligence.

4. Test results indicate that first grade children who come from a bilingual background have a somewhat smaller understanding vocabulary estimate than those children who come from a monolingual background.

5. As a result of this study, it would appear that many educators are underestimating the size of total understanding vocabulary of first grade children.

6. Data derived as a result of this study substantiate the general size of first grade children's understanding vocabulary as estimated by Mary K. Smith in 1941.

7. It appears that the bilingual child is not sufficiently advanced in the English language to receive the same instruction on the first grade level as the average monolingual child.

8. It would seem unwise to start any but children of superior linguistic ability with a second language unnecessarily during the preschool years.

Not all vocabulary data jibe, of course. Kolson (96), working with 494 Pittsburgh, Pennsylvania; Portland, Oregon; and Washington, D. C., area kindergartners, found that ". . . the kindergarten child has a minimal vocabulary of 3,728 words" in his sample. Differences in procedures change outcomes, as does a difference of one year in age, but the Shibles and Kolson studies nonetheless seem to be somewhat in conflict with respect to the words five- and six-year-olds possess. Much of the discrepancy may reside in the distinction between words *used* (Kolson study) and words *recognized when one is tested* (Shibles study).

A Payne Fund Communication Project financed the Dale-Eichholz (41) children's word knowledge study, for which an interim (1954-60) report has been released. Children in grades four, six, eight, ten, and twelve participated in work leading to the compilation of a list of 25,000 words known to at least two-thirds of the pupils. By 1960, 700 schools in 42 states were represented in the massive Dale-Eichholz investigation. Loeb (104) selected a much smaller Arkansas sample of 60 boys and girls in grades four, five, and six. His results showed relationships between vocabulary and both I.Q. and socioeconomic status, but not with respect to sex. The levels of parents' education, but not the presence of radio and TV in the home, correlated positively with the size of vocabularies their children possessed. Also, children with good vocabularies had good attitudes toward reading.

Fry (56) in 1960 discussed a list of 300 so-called instant words, said to be more than half of the total number children encounter during the first three years of their experience with reading texts. The author also suggested devices that proved useful in teaching reading. In an earlier 1957 article, Fry (55) introduced all 600 of his instant words and commented on their value in remedial reading.

Vocabularies and textbooks. Reeve (137) has analyzed the vocabularies in seven widely sold primary reader series and noted interesting discrepancies among them. For example:

A total of 109 (out of 633 introduced) words were common to all seven; and 41 additional words appeared in six, making a total of 150 words common to six or more of the seven series.

Number of new words introduced in all the basic preprimers of the seven series totaled 115. Sixty-six or 57 percent of these words were included in the 109 common to all seven series.

Two hundred and thirty-one of the 633 different words appeared in only one of the series.

The number of words beginning with certain consonants varied.

The number of new words appearing . . . varied from 17 . . . to 64. . . .

Gates (65) reviewed vocabulary control in basal reading material, while Spache (170) dealt with reading in various content fields. Staiger's (175) examination of certain language factors in the readability of primary reading textbooks also is of interest. He identified, in the list which follows, ten factors which appeared to influence readability at the primary level:

1. Syllabic length of words
2. Words typically introduced in Second Readers
3. Words typically introduced in First Readers
4. Running words in the Dale List of 769 "Easy Words"
5. Monosyllabic words

6. Different words on the Dale List of 769 "Easy Words"
7. Different words on the Thorndike List of 500 Commonest Words
8. Words typically introduced in Third Readers
9. Different words among the Thorndike 1,000 Commonest Words
10. Words per paragraph.

Particular attention must be directed to the Strickland (184) study, which created nationwide interest upon its publication in the summer of 1962, including comment in such major magazines as *Newsweek*. Entitled descriptively *The Language of Elementary School Children: Its Relationship to the Language of Reading Textbooks and the Quality of Reading of Selected Children,* the substantial 131-page Strickland bulletin was funded through a United States Office of Education contract.

The research was designed to answer the following five major questions (184:101):

1. What patterns of structure appear in the oral language used by children in the six grades of the elementary school?

2. What patterns of subordination and elaboration can be isolated and described through linguistic analysis?

3. To what extent are these patterns of structure found in the language of children at each of the six grade levels related to the variables of age, sex, and intelligence of the children and the socio-economic background and education of the parents?

4. Are the language patterns which children use at these grade levels (Grades 1 through 6) found in the reading textbooks designed for these grades?

5. What relationships appear at sixth grade level between the structure of children's oral language and their silent reading comprehension, oral reading interpretation, and listening comprehension?

Space limitations preclude reproducing more than the following concluding statement (184:106) from Strickland:

The value of this research resides mainly in the evidence it has produced regarding the patterns of linguistic structure commonly used by children and the tremendous flexibility with which children use these patterns in their oral language. It seems safe to say that children learn fairly thoroughly at an early age the basic structures of their language.

The oral language children use is far more advanced than the language of the books in which they are taught to read. Perhaps this is as it should be, but evidence is needed as to whether children would be aided or hindered by the use of sentences in their books more like the sentences they use in their speech.

It is possible that children need help to recognize and understand the entire phonemic scheme of English, not only the basic phonemes that are built into morphemes but also the suprasegmental phonemes of pitch, stress, and juncture as they use them in oral speech. Such knowledge might help children better to turn the stimulus of printed symbols into oral language patterns for both comprehension and interpretation.

No evidence is available regarding the relationship which may exist between children's use of basic structural patterns and the degree of grammaticalness of their speech. It may be that help with recognizing by ear, tongue, and mind the basic structural patterns of English and their interrelationship will help with the teaching of grammar and usage.

Reading and Listening

Since listening (auding) is discussed elsewhere in this monograph (cf. Chapter Eight), the research mentioned here is deliberately restricted.

A study by Hampleman (79) added appreciably to Young's (207) 1936 Iowa investigation of the relation of reading comprehension/retention and hearing comprehension/retention. The Hampleman project, made in eight Illinois schools, drew on 490 pupils in grades four and six. Findings included the eight listed here:

1. The data indicate that the sixth grade pupils were significantly superior to the fourth grade pupils in both listening and reading comprehension.

2. Listening comprehension was found to be significantly superior to reading comprehension for fourth grade pupils and sixth grade pupils of both sexes.

3. Easy material is more readily comprehended than hard material by fourth grade pupils and sixth grade pupils of both sexes.

4. Listening comprehension for fourth and sixth grade pupils shows a greater superiority over reading comprehension with easy material than with hard material.

5. In comprehending the hard material the boys were superior to the girls in this study.

6. Varying the length of passages of story-type material produced no apparent differences in the ability to comprehend such passages.

7. The relationship between listening and reading comprehension does not appear to be altered by the length of the passage.

8. An increase in mental age decreases the differences between listening and reading comprehension.

Rockville, New York, was the site of another listening and reading achievement experiment. The purpose of this project carried out by Kelty (93) was to determine the effect that training in listening for certain purposes had upon the ability of a group of fourth grade pupils to read for these same purposes. These purposes were (a) deciding upon the main idea of a selection, (b) deciding upon the supporting details given in a selection, and (c) drawing a conclusion.

Based on her work in four schools with 188 fourth graders, Kelty reached (among others) the conclusion that training in listening has a positive but not particularly significant effect on reading to note details. This was also true with regard to training in listening as an aid in deciding upon a main idea and in drawing a conclusion.

Physiology and Reading

The heading for this section is used loosely in order to encompass a wide range of inquiries at least indirectly concerned with physical elements in the reading process.

Physical development and reading. In the realm of physical development, Nally (115) noted that ". . . height appears to bear a predictive relationship to reading incipiency. . . ." Gilbert (69) studied the eye movements of second graders, and with consummate patience, followed up this work when the same children were senior classmen in the university. While all his subjects made progress, ". . . there was a marked tendency for those who were very slow in fixation pauses in second grade to continue so in college."

Schubert (160), seeking to locate relationships between visual maturity and success in reading in the early grades, stated that "Reading is a visual skill of the highest order." He also reviewed medical opinion suggesting that many children are expected to read too soon under conditions that are inconsistent with their visual development.

Of interest to those concerned with the physiology of reading is the Leavell-Beck (100) analysis of visual dominance and reading success and Frazier's (54) painstaking study of children's autonomic physiological reactions while reading materials at various levels of difficulty. Respiration rate, heartbeat, galvanic skin response, and blood pressure were recorded. Findings plainly indicated that varied levels of difficulty in reading material created pronounced physical responses. Smith (167), in a survey of the literature, also has documented the emotional impact of reading. "Emotional disturbances," she said, "may cause reading difficulties or vice versa, both usually being the result of a constellation of causes."

Still in the realm of physiology, broadly construed, is Fennema's (50) work with respect to mental imagery and reading. She has preserved interesting data as to the nature of the imagery of 39 Wisconsin children. Plattor *et al.* (129) worked on retardation and intelligence at the seventh grade level, adding to the general consensus that purportedly low I.Q.s may really be reflections of reading retardation.

Sex differences. The conclusion that sex has a bearing on level-of-performance in reading at certain grade levels has been suggested by a number of research studies. Recent publications by Prescott (131) and Gates (63) further confirm earlier conclusions. Using large samples, both men found that girls are likely to outperform boys in reading in the elementary school. Of slight consolation to males was Prescott's conclusion that *average* boys did a bit better than *average* girls on the tests he used.

Gates studied 13,114 pupils in grades two to eight to report on the fact of female superiority as recently as 1961. The young ladies excelled in both speed and vocabulary. One shred of consolation for the lads: some of the very best reading scores were sometimes made by males!

Difficult to classify . . . A few "physiological" studies do not fit well into usual categories. Among these are Staiger's (177) use of "Deanol" with retarded readers. This medicine, when taken by an experimental group, led to no statistically significant difference in the reading ability of experimental and control groups in any event.

Tinker (189) investigated the influence of nonhorizontal alignment of printed lines and inferred that the angle at which such lines are read should not deviate markedly from the horizontal lest it reduce reading speed and impair visibility.

Personality factors as influences on reading comprehension were explored by Chronister (32). Among his findings were the points that the personality factors he measured in Missouri children only slightly influenced comprehension and that ". . . intelligence appeared to be more significant than any of the personality factors studied."

Miscellaneous Studies of Interest

A few miscellaneous reports directly or peripherally related to reading bring this résumé of current and recent research to a close.

With respect to the use of typewriters as stimulants to learning, Capehart (28) reviewed research that suggested that typewriting seems ". . . to be valuable as a teaching tool in the elementary grades; but, reports of research and experiments do not agree on how much it improves learning, when it should be introduced, what materials are best, what methods are most effective, or who should teach it."

Study-skills courses were surveyed and found helpful by Entwisle (49), and Stone (180) endeavored constructively to criticize Spache's word list in establishing a readability scale at the primary level.

In an entertaining vein, Anderson (4) found modern basal readers to be at least as replete with moral values as McGuffey's vaunted and vintage texts. Dilley (45) endeavored to determine whether children exposed to deliberately misspelled words in trade names were hindered in learning to read and spell. Happily, no serious damage appears to have been done!

Blakely (12) gave a reasonably clean bill of health to the ubiquitous comic book by finding (at least insofar as 281 seventh graders were concerned) that his data did not ". . . support curtailment of children's access to comic books." Addicts to the comic books were getting along as well in school as were the abstainers.

Schools attended at the secondary level, parents' occupational status, and the student's age were identified by Newton (119) as major indices of success in reading at the college level.

Summary

Research in reading continues to create an interesting mosaic of conflict, consensus, and contribution. During the past six or seven years a steady stream of articles and reports have added to our fund of knowledge with regard to reading while at the same time raising more questions than have been settled.

Writings reflect increased public interest in improved instruction, and as if in response, research reports seem to have concentrated a bit more successfully on better ways of improving professional methods and procedures.

On the whole, while uneven, the picture is a good one when seen in perspective. Instruction seems to be improving a shade more rapidly, information is available in more sources, and the area is somewhat more crisply delineated than, say, in 1955.

A good index to the dynamism of the present, not only in reading but in the language arts as a whole, was provided by Early and Strom (46) in their 1960-61 summary of research for this brief period. Early felt that a number of studies lack vigor, while Strom advanced the well-taken point that many reports are static rather than *dynamic*. Nevertheless, increased public interest and more available research monies seem to hold a measure of promise for continued improvement in the processes of professional inquiry as they relate to reading.

Bibliography

1. AARON, IRA E.; FRANCES GOODWIN; and VADA KENT. "Fourth Grade Teachers Experiment with Cross-Class Grouping for Reading Instruction." *Elementary English* 36:305-307; May 1959.

2. AHMANN, JOHN STANLEY, and MARVIN D. GLOCK. "The Utility of Study Habits and Attitudes Inventory in a College Reading Program." *Journal of Educational Research* 51:297-303; December 1957.

3. ANDERSON, A. W. "Personality Traits in Reading Ability of Western Australian University Freshmen." *Journal of Educational Research* 54:234-37; February 1961.

4. ANDERSON, PAUL S. "McGuffey vs. the Moderns in Character Training." *Phi Delta Kappan* 38:53-58; November 1956.

5. ARTLEY, STERL A. "Critical Reading in the Content Areas." *Elementary English* 41:122-29; February 1959.

6. BARBE, WALTER B. "Reading Improvement and Group Intelligence Test Scores." *School and Society* 82:72-73; September 3, 1955.

7. BEAR, DAVID E. "Phonics for First Grade: A Comparison of Two Methods." *Elementary School Journal* 59:394-402; April 1959.

8. BERNSTEIN, MARGERY R. "Relationship Between Interest and Reading Comprehension." *Journal of Educational Research* 49:283-88; December 1955.

9. BETTS, EMMETT ALBERT. "How Well Are We Teaching Reading?" *Elementary English* 38:371-81; October 1961.

10. BETTS, EMMETT ALBERT. "Reading and the Fourth R." *Elementary English* 35:18-25; January 1958.

11. BETTS, EMMETT ALBERT. "Reading Is Thinking." *Education Digest* 24:47-49; May 1959.

12. BLAKELY, W. PAUL. "A Study of Seventh-Grade Children's Reading of Comic Books as Related to Certain Other Variables." *Journal of Genetic Psychology* 93:291-301; December 1958.

13. BLAKELY, W. PAUL, and ERMA M. SHADLE. "A Study of Two Readiness for Reading Programs in Kindergarten." *Elementary English* 38:502-505; November 1961.

14. BLIESMER, EMERY P. "A Comparison of Results of Various Capacity Tests Used with Retarded Readers." *Elementary School Journal* 56:400-402; May 1956.

15. BLIESMER, EMERY P. "1959 Review of Research on College and Non-College Adult Reading." *Research and Evaluation in College Reading.* Ninth Yearbook of the National Reading Conference. Fort Worth: Texas Christian University Press, 1960. p. 49-62.

16. BLIESMER, EMERY P., and ALVIN J. LOWE. "1960 Review of Research on College and Non-College Adult Reading." *Phases of College and Other Adult Reading Programs.* Tenth Yearbook of the National Reading Conference. Milwaukee: Reading Center, Marquette University, 1961. p. 150-70.

17. BLOOMER, RICHARD H. "Concepts of Meaning and the Reading and Spelling Difficulty of Words." *Journal of Educational Research* 54:178-82; January 1961.

18. BLOOMER, RICHARD H. "Connotative Meaning and the Reading and Spelling Difficulty of Words." *Journal of Educational Research* 55:107-12; November 1961.

19. BLOOMER, RICHARD H. "Level of Abstraction as a Function of Modifier Load." *Journal of Educational Research* 52:269-72; March 1959.

20. BOHNHORST, BEN A., and SOPHIA N. SELLARS. "Individual Reading Instruction vs. Basal Textbook Instruction: Some Tentative Explorations." *Elementary English* 36:185-90, 202; March 1959.

21. BOND, GUY L., and THEODORE CLYMER. "Interrelationship of the SRA Primary Mental Abilities, Other Mental Characteristics, and Reading Abilities." *Journal of Educational Research* 49:131-36; October 1955.

22. BOTTOMLY, FORBES. "An Experiment with the Controlled Reader." *Journal of Educational Research* 54:265-69; March 1961.

23. BOUTWELL, WILLIAM DOW. "What's Happening in Education?" *PTA Magazine* 55:14-15; June 1961.

24. BRADLEY, BEATRICE E. "An Experimental Study of the Readiness Approach to Reading." *Elementary School Journal* 56:262-67; February 1956.

25. BREMER, NEVILLE E. "Do Readiness Tests Predict Success in Reading?" *Elementary School Journal* 59:222-24; January 1959.

26. BREMER, NEVILLE E. "First-Grade Achievement Under Different Plans of Grouping." *Elementary English* 35:324-26; May 1958.

27. BURKE, VIRGINIA M. "A Candid Opinion on Lay Readers." *English Journal* 50:258-64; April 1961.

28. CAPEHART, BERTIS E. *Does the Portable Typewriter Stimulate Learning in the Elementary School Classroom?* New York: Education Department, Hill and Knowlton, Inc., 1959. 14 p.

29. CARROLL, JOHN B. "The Case of Dr. Flesch." *American Psychologist* 11:158-63; March 1956.

30. CARSON, LOUISE G. "Moving Toward Individualization—A Second Grade Program." *Elementary English* 34:362-66; October 1957.

31. CHANSKY, NORMAN M., and MARTIN BREGMAN. "Improvement of Reading in College." *Journal of Educational Research* 51:313-17; December 1957.

32. CHRONISTER, GLENN MORRISON. "A Study of the Ability of Measures of Certain Aspects of Personality To Differentiate Between Boys' and Girls' Success in Reading." *Dissertations in Education.* Columbia: University of Missouri Bulletin, Study 13, 1961. p. 39-41.

33. GORDON, IRA J. (University of Florida), and CHRISTINE H. CLARK (Alachau County Schools, Florida). "An Experiment in Individualized Reading." *Childhood Education* 38:112-13; November 1961.

34. CLELAND, DORIS I., and JOSEPHINE T. BENSON, editors. *Corrective and Remedial Reading.* A Report of the Sixteenth Annual Conference and Course on Reading. Pittsburgh: University of Pittsburgh, 1960. 213 p.

35. CLYMER, THEODORE. *The Utility of Phonic Generalizations in the Primary Grades.* An informal research paper presented to IRA-NCRE meeting, St. Louis, May 5, 1961. 15 p. Mimeographed.

36. CLYMER. THEODORE, and HELEN M. ROBINSON. "Reading Comprehension." *Review of Educational Research* 31:130-34; April 1961.

37. CONDIT, MARTHA O. "Trade Books for Beginning Readers." *Wilson Library Bulletin* 34:284-301; December 1959.

38. COOK, DESMOND L. "A Comparison of Reading Comprehension Scores Obtained Before and After a Time Announcement." *Journal of Educational Psychology* 48:440-46; November 1957.

39. COSPER, RUSSELL, and NEWELL C. KEPHART. "Retention of Reading Skills." *Journal of Educational Research* 49:211-16; November 1955.

40. CROSBY, MURIEL ESTELLE. "Experience and the Reading Process." *Elementary English* 36:552-55; December 1959.

41. DALE, EDGAR, and GERALD EICHHOLZ. *Children's Knowledge of Words, An Interim Report (September 1954 to June 1960).* A Payne Fund Communication Project. Columbus: Bureau of Educational Research and Service, The Ohio State University, 1960. n. p.

42. DALE, EDGAR, and DONALD REICHERT. *Bibliography of Vocabulary Studies.* Revised edition. Columbus: Bureau of Educational Research and Service, The Ohio State University, 1957. 174 p.

43. DANIELS, JOHN CLIFFORD, and HUNTER DIACK. "Phonic Word Method." *Education Digest* 25:45-47; January 1960.

44. DIACK, HUNTER. *Reading and the Psychology of Perception.* New York: Philosophical Library, Inc., 1960. 155 p.

45. DILLEY, NORMAN EDWARD. "Trade Names and the Learning of Spelling and Reading." *Elementary English* 35:226-29; April 1958.

46. EARLY, MARGARET, and INGRID STROM. *A Summary of Research in the English Language Arts—Elementary and Secondary, 1960-1961.* Reprinted from *Elementary English* and *English Journal.* Champaign, Illinois: National Council of Teachers of English, 508 South Sixth Street, n.d. 32 p.

47. EDWARDS, D. LEWIS. "Reading from the Child's Point of View." *Elementary English* 35:239-41; April 1958.

48. ELLER, WILLIAM, and ROBERT DYKSTRA. "Persuasion and Personality: Readers' Predispositions as a Factor in Critical Reading." *Elementary English* 36:191-97, 202; March 1959.

49. ENTWISLE, DORIS R. "Evaluations of Study-Skills Courses: A Review." *Journal of Educational Research* 53:243-51; March 1960.

50. FENNEMA, ELIZABETH H. "Mental Imagery and the Reading Process." *Elementary School Journal* 59:286-89; February 1959.

51. FJELDSTED, LILLIAN W. "Broadening Reading Interest Through Creative Expression." *Elementary English* 35:391-94; October 1958.

52. FLESCH, RUDOLPH. *Why Johnny Can't Read.* New York: Harper and Brothers, 1955. 222 p.

53. FORD, PAUL M. "Lay Readers in the High School Composition Program: Some Statistics." *English Journal* 50:522-28; November 1961.

54. FRAZIER, ELIZABETH. "A Study of Certain Autonomic Physiological Reactions of Selected Children Reading at Various Levels of Difficulty." *Dissertations in Education.* Columbia: University of Missouri Bulletin, Study 20, 1957. p. 40-41.

55. FRY, EDWARD B. "Developing a Word List for Remedial Reading." *Elementary English* 34:456-58; November 1957.

56. FRY, EDWARD B. "Teaching a Basic Reading Vocabulary." *Elementary English* 37:38-42; January 1960.

57. GATES, ARTHUR I. "A Review of *Tomorrow's Illiterates,* by Charles E. Walcutt, and *What Ivan Knows That Johnny Doesn't,* by Arthur S. Trace, Jr." 23 p. Mimeographed.

58. GATES, ARTHUR I. *The Age of Teaching Beginning Reading.* New York 27: Associated Public School Systems, 525 West 120th Street, n.d. 5 p. Mimeographed.

59. GATES, ARTHUR I. "Controversies About Teaching Reading." Manuscript in preparation (Spring 1962) for publication in *School and Society.* 6 p. Mimeographed.

60. GATES, ARTHUR I. "Fulminations About Phonics." *Educational Forum* 25:523-28; May 1961.

61. GATES, ARTHUR I. "The Future of Research in Reading." *Education* 82:545-54; May 1962.

62. GATES, ARTHUR I. "News and Comment: Teaching Machines in Perspective." *Elementary School Journal* 62:1-13; October 1961.

63. GATES, ARTHUR I. "Sex Differences in Reading Ability." *Elementary School Journal* 61:431-34; May 1961.

64. GATES, ARTHUR I. "The Teaching of Reading—Objective Evidence Versus Opinion." *Phi Delta Kappan* 43:197-205; February 1962.

65. GATES, ARTHUR I. "Vocabulary Control in Basal Reading Material." *Reading Teacher* 15:81-85; November 1961.

66. GATES, ARTHUR I. "What We Know and Can Do About the Poor Reader." *Education* 77:528-33; May 1957.

67. GATES, ARTHUR I. (Teachers College), and GUY L. BOND (Speyer Experimental School). "Reading Readiness: A Study of Factors in Beginning Reading." *Teachers College Record* 37:679-85; May 1936.

68. GEBOE, JUANITA. "Folklore for Superior Readers in Third Grade." *Elementary English* 37:93-97; February 1960.

69. GILBERT, LUTHER C. "Genetic Study of Eye Movements in Reading." *Elementary School Journal* 59:328-35; March 1959.

70. GOINS, JEAN TURNER. "Visual Perceptual Abilities and Early Reading Progress." *Supplementary Educational Monographs,* No. 87. Chicago: University of Chicago Press, February 1958. 108 p.

71. GRAY, WILLIAM S. "Current Reading Problems: A World View." *Elementary School Journal* 56:11-17; September 1955.

72. GRAY, WILLIAM S. "Reading." *Encyclopedia of Educational Research.* Chester W. Harris, editor. Third edition. New York: The Macmillan Company, 1960. p. 1086-1135.

73. GRAY, WILLIAM S. "Summary of Reading Investigations July 1, 1955 to June 30, 1956." *Journal of Educational Research* 50:401-41; February 1957.

74. GRAY, WILLIAM S. "Summary of Reading Investigations July 1, 1956 to June 30, 1957." *Journal of Educational Research* 51:401-35; February 1958.

75. GRAY, WILLIAM S. "Summary of Reading Investigations July 1, 1957 to June 30, 1958." *Journal of Educational Research* 52:203-21; February 1959.

76. GRAY, WILLIAM S. "Summary of Investigations Relating to Reading July 1, 1958 to June 30, 1959." *Journal of Educational Research* 53:203-22; February 1960.

77. GRISSOM, LOREN V. "Characteristics of Successful Reading Improvement Programs." *English Journal* 50:461-64, 474; October 1961.

78. GROFF, PATRICK J. "Librarian and Individualized Reading." *Wilson Library Bulletin* 34:359-61; January 1960.

79. HAMPLEMAN, RICHARD S. "Comparison of Listening and Reading Comprehension Ability of Fourth and Sixth Grade Pupils." Unpublished doctoral thesis. Bloomington: School of Education, Indiana University, 1955. 171 p. Typed.

80. HANITCHAK, JOHN J. "Oral Peak Stress: Its Validity and Relationship to Reading Comprehension and Efficiency." *Journal of Educational Research* 52:228-31; February 1959.

81. HART, RICHARD H. "The Effectiveness of an Approach to the Problem of Varying Abilities in Teaching Reading." *Journal of Educational Research* 49:295-99; December 1955.

82. HAUGH, OSCAR M. "Research in Reading at the University of Kansas." *Teaching Reading in the High School.* Kansas Studies in Education, Vol. 10, No. 1. Lawrence: School of Education, University of Kansas, February 1960. p. 33-46.

83. HILL, EDWIN H. "Effect of Television on Children's Reading Habits." *Conference on Reading.* Pittsburgh: University of Pittsburgh, 1958. p. 165-73.

84. HOGENSON, DENNIS L. "Public Library, Ally of the Reading Teacher." *Library Journal* 85:328-29; January 15, 1960.

85. HOGENSON, DENNIS L. "Role of Interest in Improving Reading Skills." *Elementary English* 37:244-46; April 1960.

86. HOYT, JEANNE S., and DOROTHY S. BLACKMORE. "Fifty Seventh Graders: A Comparison of Their Reading Achievement and Expected Achievement in Grades One Through Seven." *Journal of Educational Research* 53:163-71; January 1960.

87. THE INSTITUTE OF STUDENT OPINION. "Student Reading Habits." *English Journal* 49:499; October 1960.

88. JOHNSON, MARJORIE S. "A Study of Diagnostic and Remedial Procedures in a Reading Clinic Laboratory School." *Journal of Educational Research* 48:565-78; April 1955.

89. KARLIN, ROBERT. "Machines and Reading: A Review of Research." *Clearing House* 32:349-52; February 1958.

90. KARLIN, ROBERT. "Physical Growth and Success in Undertaking Beginning Reading." *Journal of Educational Research* 51:191-201; November 1957.

91. KARLIN, ROBERT. "The Prediction of Reading Success and Reading Readiness Tests." *Elementary English* 34:320-25; May 1957.

92. KELLY, BARBARA CLINE. "The Economy Method Versus the Scott Foresman Method in Teaching Second-Grade Reading in the Murphysboro Public Schools." *Journal of Educational Research* 51:465-69; February 1958.

93. KELTY, ANNETTE P. "An Experimental Study To Determine the Effect of 'Listening for Certain Purposes' upon Achievement in Reading for These Purposes." *Abstracts of Field Studies for the Degree of Doctor of Education,* Vol. 15. Greeley: Colorado State College of Education, 1954. p. 82-85.

94. KINGSLEY, MARJORIE. "An Experiment in Individualized Reading." *Elementary English* 35:113-18; February 1958.

95. KINGSTON, ALBERT J., and CLAY E. GEORGE. "The Effectiveness of Reading Training at the College Level." *Journal of Educational Research* 48:467-71; February 1955.

96. KOLSON, CLIFFORD JOHN. "The Vocabulary of Kindergarten Children." Unpublished doctoral thesis. Pittsburgh: University of Pittsburgh, 1960. 152 p. Typed.

97. KOVAS, HELEN. "The Place of Oral Reading." *Elementary English* 34:462-66; November 1957.

98. LARRICK, NANCY. "What Parents Think About Children's Reading." *Elementary English* 33:206-10; April 1956.

99. LARSON, ROBERT E., and CYNTHIA T. SELLAND. "A Comparison of Reading Ages with Mental Ages." *Journal of Educational Research* 52:55-59; October 1958.

100. LEAVELL, ULLIN W., and HARRY S. BECK. "Ability of Retarded Readers To Recognize Symbols in Association with Lateral Dominance." *Peabody Journal of Education* 37:7-14; July 1959.

101. LETSON, CHARLES T. "The Relative Influence of Material and Purpose on Reading Rates." *Journal of Educational Research* 52:238-40; February 1959.

102. LETSON, CHARLES T. "Speed and Comprehension in Reading." *Journal of Educational Research* 52:49-53; October 1958.

103. LICHTENSTEIN, JACK. "New Castle Reading Experiment in Cleveland Heights." *Elementary English* 37:27-28; January 1960.

104. LOEB, JOE H. "A Vocabulary Study of 4th, 5th, and 6th Grade Children." *Dissertation Abstracts* 17:1494-95; July 1957.

105. McCULLOUGH, CONSTANCE M. "Responses of Elementary School Children to Common Types of Reading Comprehension Questions." *Journal of Educational Research* 51:65-70; September 1957.

106. MANLEY, DOROTHY J.; MARY BUTTI; and ELI JACOBSON. "Let's Fight Reading Retardation." *High Points* 41:34-46; December 1959.

107. MASSEY, WILLIAM JOSEPH. "The Development of the Modern Sequential Program of Word Perception as Revealed by the Literature." *Dissertations in Education.* Columbia: University of Missouri Bulletin, Study 30; 1955.

108. MILLER, VERA V., and WENDELL C. LANTON. "Reading Achievement of School Children—Then and Now." *Elementary English* 33:91-97; February 1956.

109. MILLMAN, CHARLOTTE L. "An Individualized Reading Program." *Elementary English* 35:386-88; October 1958.

110. MILLS, ROBERT E. "An Evaluation of Techniques for Teaching Word Recognition." *Elementary School Journal* 56:221-25; January 1956.

111. MINGOIA, EDWIN. "Helping Unsuccessful Students." *Clearing House* 35:471-74; April 1961.

112. MOE, IVER L. "Auding as a Predictive Measure of Reading Performance in Primary Grades." Unpublished doctoral thesis. Gainesville: University of Florida, 1957. 128 p. Typed.

113. MORRONE, VICTOR EUGENE. "A Critical Analysis of Scientific Research in Phonics." Unpublished doctoral thesis. Pittsburgh: University of Pittsburgh, 1958. 197 p. Typed.

114. MULDER, ROBERT L., and JAMES CURTIN. "Vocal Phonic Ability and Silent Reading Achievement: A First Report." *Elementary School Journal* 56:121-23; November 1955.

115. NALLY, THOMAS P. F. "The Relationship Between Achieved Growth in Height and the Beginning Growth in Reading." *Journal of Educational Research* 49:153-54; October 1955.

116. NATIONAL CONFERENCE ON RESEARCH IN READING. *Needed Research in Reading.* Prepared by the Sub-Committee on Needed Research; n.d. 5 p. Mimeographed.

117. NEVILLE, DONALD. "A Comparison of the WISC Patterns of Male Retarded and Nonretarded Readers." *Journal of Educational Research* 54:195-97; January 1961.

118. NEVILLE, MARK A. "Methods for Improving Appreciation of Materials Presented Orally in Grades Seven Through Nine." *Conference on Reading.* Chicago: University of Chicago, 1955. p. 116-20.

119. NEWTON, EUNICE SHAED. "Empirical Differences Between Adequate and Retarded Readers." *Reading Teacher* 13:40-44; October 1959.

120. NORVELL, GEORGE W. "Developing Reading Interests and Attitudes Among Adolescents." *Reading in the Content Areas.* A Report of the Fifteenth Annual Conference and Course on Reading. Pittsburgh: University of Pittsburgh, 1959. p. 137-47.

121. NORVELL, GEORGE W. "The Reading Interests of Children." *Reading in the Content Areas.* A Report of the Fifteenth Annual Conference and Course on Reading. Pittsburgh: University of Pittsburgh, 1959. p. 125-35.

122. PAUK, WALTER J. "Are Present Reading Tests Valid for Both Girls and Boys?" *Journal of Educational Research* 53:279-80; March 1960.

123. PELLER, LILI. "Reading and Daydreams in Latency, Boy-Girl Differences." *Journal of the American Psychoanalytic Association* 6:57-70; January 1958.

124. PERRODIN, ALEX F. "Televiewing, Reading Habits, and Children's Social Values." *Elementary English* 37:86-90; February 1960.

125. PERRY, WILLIAM G., JR. "Students' Use and Misuse of Reading Skills: A Report to a Faculty." *Harvard Educational Review,* Vol. 29, No. 3; Summer 1959. p. 193-200.

126. PETTY, WALTER T. "Critical Reading in the Primary Grades." *Elementary English* 33:302-306; May 1956.

127. PICKARZ, JOSEPHINE A. "Getting Meaning from Reading." *Elementary School Journal* 56:303-309; March 1956.

128. PITKANEN, ALLAN M. "Inadequate Readers in the Classroom." *Clearing House* 35:357-61; May 1961.

129. PLATTOR, EMMA E., and OTHERS. "Relationship Between Reading Retardation and the Measurement of Intelligence." *Personnel and Guidance Journal* 38:49-51; September 1959.

130. POOLEY, ROBERT C. "Reading and the Language Arts." *Development in and Through Reading.* Nelson B. Henry, editor. Sixteenth Yearbook of the National Society for the Study of Education, Part 1. Chicago: University of Chicago Press, 1960. p. 35-53.

131. PRESCOTT, GEORGE A. "Sex Differences in Metropolitan Readiness Tests Results." *Journal of Educational Research* 48:605-10; April 1955.

132. PRESNALL, HUGO E. "Parents' Opinions of Reading Instruction." *Elementary English* 33:29-33; January 1956.

133. PRINCE, J. W. "Meaning for the Masses." *Elementary English* 38:308-15; May 1961.

134. RAMSAY, WALLACE Z. "An Experiment in Teaching Reading in High School English Classes." *English Journal* 46:495-500; November 1957.

135. RANSON, M. KATHLEEN. "An Evaluation of Certain Aspects of the Reading and Study Programs at the University of Missouri." *Journal of Educational Research* 48:443-54; February 1955.

136. RAYMOND, DOROTHY M. "The Performance of Reading Achievers on Memory Span and Associative Learning Tests." *Journal of Educational Research* 48:455-65; February 1955.

137. REEVE, OLIVE R. "The Vocabulary of Seven Primary Reading Series." *Elementary English* 35:237-39; April 1958.

138. REEVES, RUTH E. "Experiment in Improving Reading in the Junior High School." *English Journal* 47:15-20; January 1958.

139. REPP, FLORENCE C. "The Vocabularies of Five Recent Third Grade Arithmetic Textbooks." *Arithmetic Teacher* 7:128-32; March 1960.

140. ROBERTS, RICHARD W., and JAMES C. COLEMAN. "An Investigation of the Role of Visual and Kinesthetic Factors in Reading Failure." *Journal of Educational Research* 51:445-51; February 1958.

141. ROBINSON, H. ALAN, and DAN S. DRAMER. "High School Reading—1960." *Journal of Developmental Reading* 5:3-14; Autumn 1961.

142. ROBINSON, HELEN M. "Can Retarded Readers Develop Permanent Interest in Reading?" *Reading Teacher* 12:235-39; April 1959.

143. ROBINSON, HELEN M. "Development of Reading Skills." *Elementary School Journal* 58:269-74; February 1958.

144. ROBINSON, HELEN M. "Factors Which Affect Success in Reading." *Elementary School Journal* 55:263-69; January 1955.

145. ROBINSON, HELEN M., editor. "Reading Instruction in Various Patterns of Grouping." *Supplementary Educational Monographs,* No. 89. Chicago: University of Chicago Press, 1959. 212 p.

146. ROBINSON, HELEN M., editor. "Sequential Development of Reading Abilities." *Supplementary Educational Monographs,* No. 90. Chicago: University of Chicago Press, 1960. 251 p.

147. ROBINSON, HELEN M. "Summary of Investigations Relating to Reading July 1, 1959 to June 30, 1960." *Journal of Educational Research* 54:203-20; February 1961.

148. ROWLETT, JUDY. "Let's Re-Emphasize Some Neglected Skills." *Peabody Journal of Education* 32:327-28; May 1955.

149. RUDISILL, MABEL F. "Interrelations of Functional Phonic Knowledge, Reading, Spelling, and Mental Age." *Elementary School Journal* 57:264-67; February 1957.

150. RUSSELL, DAVID H. "An Evaluation of Some Easy-To-Read Trade Books for Children." *Elementary English* 38:475-82; November 1961.

151. RUSSELL, DAVID H. "Personal Values in Reading." *Reading Teacher* 12:3-9, October 1958.

152. RUSSELL, DAVID H. "Primary Reading Programs in England and Scotland." *Elementary School Journal* 57:446-51; May 1957.

153. RUSSELL, DAVID H. "Progress in Reading: A Special Review." *Elementary English* 37:242-44; April 1957.

154. RUSSELL, DAVID H. "Reading Research That Makes a Difference." *Elementary English* 38:74-78; February 1961.

155. RUSSELL, DAVID H. "Some Research on the Impact of Reading." *English Journal* 47:398-413; October 1958.

156. RUSSELL, DAVID H., and PATRICK J. GROFF. "Personal Factors Influencing Perception in Reading." *Education* 75:600-603; May 1955.

157. SARTAIN, HARRY W. "A Bibliography on Individualized Reading." *Reading Teacher* 13:262-65, 270; April 1960.

158. SARTAIN, HARRY W. "The Roseville Experiment with Individualized Reading." *Reading Teacher* 13:277-81; April 1960.

159. SCHICK, GEORGE B. "Reading and the Language Arts." *Phases of College and Other Adult Reading Programs*. Tenth Yearbook of the National Reading Conference. Milwaukee: Reading Center, Marquette University, 1961. p. 58-67.

160. SCHUBERT, DELWYN G. "Visual Immaturity and Reading Difficulty." *Elementary English* 34:323-25; May 1957.

161. SHANE, HAROLD G. "We Can Be Proud of the Facts." Freedman and Cotter. *Issues of the Sixties*. San Francisco: Wadsworth Publishing Company, Inc., 1961. p. 263ff.

162. SHELDON, WILLIAM. "Reading: Instruction." *Review of Educational Research* 25:92-106; April 1955.

163. SHIBLES, BURLEIGH H. "How Many Words Does a First-Grade Child Know?" *Elementary English* 41:42-47; January 1959.

164. SISTER JOSEPHINA. "Survey of the Research Related to the Reading Ability of the Gifted." *Journal of Educational Research* 53:237-39; February 1960.

165. SMITH, EDGAR A. "Devereux Readability Index." *Journal of Educational Research* 54:298-303; April 1961.

166. SMITH, MARY L., and ISABEL V. ENO. "What Do They Really Read?" *English Journal* 50:343-45; May 1961.

167. SMITH, NILA B. "Research on Reading and the Emotions." *School and Society* 81:8-10; January 8, 1955.

168. SMITH, NILA B. "What Have We Accomplished in Reading?—A Review of the Past Fifty Years." *Elementary English* 38:141-50; March 1961.

169. SMITH, NILA B. "What Research Tells Us About Word Recognition." *Elementary School Journal* 55:440-46; April 1955.

170. SPACHE, GEORGE D. "Reading in Various Curriculum Fields." *Education Digest* 23:47-49; April 1958.

171. SPACHE, GEORGE D. "Research in Reading at the University of Florida, 1950-1960." *Phases of College and Other Adult Reading Programs*. Tenth Yearbook of the National Reading Conference. Milwaukee: Reading Center, Marquette University, 1961. p. 141-49.

172. SPARKS, PAUL E., and LEO C. FAY. "An Evaluation of Two Methods of Teaching Reading." *Elementary School Journal* 57:386-90; April 1957.

173. SPENCER, PETER L., and DAVID H. RUSSELL. "Reading in Arithmetic." *Instruction in Arithmetic.* Twenty-Fifth Yearbook. Washington, D.C.: National Council of Teachers of Mathematics, 1960. p. 202-23.

174. SQUIRE, JAMES R. "Literacy and Literature." *English Journal* 49:154-60; March 1960.

175. STAIGER, RALPH C. "Certain Language Factors in the Readability of Primary Reading Textbooks." *Journal of Educational Research* 48:589-96; April 1955.

176. STAIGER, RALPH C. "Language Arts Research, 1960." *Elementary English* 38:175-86; March 1961.

177. STAIGER, RALPH C., and OTHERS. "Medicine for Reading Improvement." *Journal of Developmental Reading* 5:48-51; Autumn 1961.

178. STANDLEE, LLOYD S., and NICHOLAS A. FATTU. "Readability of Navy Publications." *Journal of Educational Research* 49:471-73; February 1956.

179. STILL, JANE S. "Evaluation of a Community Sponsored Summer Reading Program." *Elementary English* 38:342-43; May 1961.

180. STONE, CLARENCE R. "Measuring Difficulty of Primary Reading Material: A Constructive Criticism of Spache's Measure." *Elementary School Journal* 57:36-41; October 1956.

181. STORDAHL, KALMER E., and CLIFFORD M. CHRISTENSEN. "The Effect of Study Techniques on Comprehension and Retention." *Journal of Educational Research* 49:561-70; April 1956.

182. STRICKLAND, RUTH G. "Creating a Challenging Classroom Environment." *Reading Teacher* 10:72-81; December 1956.

183. STRICKLAND, RUTH G. "The Interrelationship Between Language and Reading." *Volta Review* 60:334-36; September 1958.

184. STRICKLAND, RUTH G. *The Language of Elementary School Children: Its Relationship to the Language of Reading Textbooks and the Quality of Reading of Selected Children.* Bulletin of the School of Education, Vol. 38, No. 4. Bloomington: Indiana University, July 1962. 131 p.

185. STROM, INGRID M. "Summary of Investigations Relating to the Language Arts in Secondary Education—1958-1959." *English Journal* 49:119-30; February 1960.

186. STROM, INGRID M. "Summary of Investigations Relating to the English Language Arts in Secondary Education: 1959-1960." *English Journal* 50:111-25; February 1961.

187. TEMPLIN, MILDRED C. "Phonic Knowledge and Its Relation to the Spelling and Reading Achievement of Fourth Grade Pupils." *Journal of Educational Research* 47:441-54; February 1954.

188. THOMPSON, WARREN C. "A Book-Centered Course Versus a Machine-Centered Course in Adult Reading Improvement." *Journal of Educational Research* 49:437-45; February 1956.

189. TINKER, MILES. "Effect of Angular Alignment upon Readability of Print." *Journal of Educational Psychology* 47:358-63; October 1956.

190. TINKER, MILES. "Eye Movements in Reading." *Education* 79:575-79; May 1959.

191. TRAXLER, ARTHUR E., and ANN JUNGEBLUT. *Research in Reading During Another Four Years, July 1, 1953—December 31, 1957.* New York: New York Educational Records Bureau, May 1960. 226 p.

192. TUFVANDER, ELLIS A., and MILES V. ZINTZ. "A Follow-Up Study of Pupils with Reading Difficulties." *Elementary School Journal* 58:152-56; December 1957.

193. TURNER, CARLA S. "Improving Selection of Pupils for Remedial Reading: A Report of Research." *English Journal* 50:23-33; January 1961.

194. TURNER, CARLA S. "Remedial Reading Pays Dividends in the Junior High School." *English Journal* 48:136-40, 153; March 1959.

195. ALLEN, R. VAN. "More Ways Than One." *Childhood Education* 39:108-11; November 1961.

196. VEATCH, JEANNETTE. "In Defense of Individualized Reading." *Elementary English* 37:227-34; April 1960.

197. VERNON, MAGDALEN D. "The Investigation of Reading Problems Today." Part I, "Symposium: Contributions to the Diagnosis and Remedial Treatment of Reading Difficulties." *British Journal of Educational Psychology* 30:146-54; June 1960.

198. VERNON, MAGDALEN D. "The Investigation of Reading Problems Today." Part II, "Symposium: Contributions to the Diagnosis and Remedial Treatment of Reading Difficulties." *British Journal of Educational Psychology* 30:146-54; June 1960.

199. WALCUTT, CHARLES. *Tomorrow's Illiterates: The State of Reading Instruction Today.* Boston: Little, Brown, 1961. 168 p.

200. WALKER, FREDERIC. "Evaluation of Three Methods of Teaching Reading, Seventh Grade." *Journal of Educational Research* 54:356-58; May 1961.

201. WARFORD, PHYLLIS. "Individualized Reading in First Grade." *Elementary English* 37:36-37; January 1960.

202. WILLIAMS, GERTRUDE H. "Provisions for Critical Reading in Basic Readers." *Elementary English* 36:323-31; May 1959.

203. WITT, FRANK. "Remedial Reading in the Junior High School: A Practical Report." *Elementary English* 36:35-41; January 1959.

204. WITTICK, MILDRED LETTON. "Sequential Development in Reading Interests and Tastes." *Conference on Reading.* Chicago: University of Chicago Press, 1960. p. 150-56.

205. WITTY, PAUL. "Reading Instruction—A Forward Look." *Elementary English* 38:151-64; March 1961.

206. WITTY, PAUL, and OTHERS. "Individualized Reading: A Summary and Evaluation." *Elementary English* 36:401-12, 450; October 1959.

207. YOUNG, WILLIAM E. "The Relation of Reading Comprehension and Retention to Hearing Comprehension and Retention." *Journal of Experimental Education* 5:30-39; September 1936.

Chapter Three

Improving Our Hen Tracks

AT LEAST a few readers will recall the era of penholders and steel points. In retrospect they will sympathize not only with themselves but with others who had reached the last line of a carefully written page only to have the point dig too deeply into the paper and spatter a written exercise or composition with ruinous ink blots. Today's ball-point and fountain-pen generation, as in years gone by, needs to be made aware of the compelling and rewarding experiences accompanying clear and literate writing.

Teachers' questions about handwriting. Teachers whose views were considered in preparing this report expressed concern about many questions related to handwriting: (a) In the light of some critical educational articles, can children or cannot children write as well as students used to write? (b) What does current research say about handwriting? (c) What do experts say about the relative merits of manuscript and cursive writing? (d) Do pressure patterns have anything to do with legibility? (e) Are speed and legibility influenced by whether children write with their right or left hands? and (f) What suggestions can be made for improving the teaching of handwriting skills? The present chapter reviews the literature related to these questions posed by teachers.

Can They or Can't They Write?

Very frequently articles are widely read when they nostalgically hark back to years past and predict that education will never be what it used to be. Nonetheless, it is fortunate that the days of rote drill with "ovals" and "push-pulls" seem to have passed with few mourners, while recognition for the importance of legible handwriting has increased.

The need for handwriting today. To determine the importance of handwriting instruction in today's schools, Templin (46) studied the script of 1946 graduates of high schools located in 20 communities in six states on the Eastern seaboard. Each graduate was sent a postcard and was asked to return the card listing those courses which he felt had proved most useful. This card was used as a handwriting sample. A questionnaire was sent also to 454 adults asking them to indicate how much and what type of writing was done by them. The following findings were among those drawn from an analysis of the questionnaires:

1. Professional workers used the most handwriting (17.7 percent per week).

2. Men (in same group) engaged in more handwriting than did women from the same group.

3. Pencils were most commonly used as writing tools.

4. Handwriting was used mainly to handle social correspondence, fill in forms, and prepare shopping lists.

5. Handwriting was used more in professional than in personal activity.

6. The typewriter has not replaced the pencil.

7. Handwriting was deemed important to efficiency in business and social world.

Indeed, it seems safe to stipulate that stress on better handwriting will remain with us for some time. Handwriting was not replaced by movable type in the years past, nor is this skill now obsolete because of other means of communication.

Some say that children can't write well . . . In 1955 Irwin's (29) article in the *Saturday Evening Post* directed attention to the prevalence of unreadable handwriting in the United States today. Irwin was motivated to write the article when Dr. William Graham, at the climax of a religious rally at Madison Square Garden, begged, "Please, my friends, please print on your cards. It will save us hours and hours of work." He was further inspired by a business executive who sharply criticized New York schools in 1953 because his ten-year-old son was learning to print rather than to use cursive writing.

Irwin cited many examples of people who lost money, missed connections, or received wrong orders, among other things, because their handwriting was illegible. He also reproduced in his article samples of handwriting that were impossible to read. Among the persons whose erratic script was shown were Adlai Stevenson, William Saroyan, William O. Douglas, and Henry D. Thoreau—none of whom had too much difficulty in communicating with vast numbers of people—nor had they attended school recently!

Hurdls (28), in a letter to the editor of the *London Times Educational Supplement,* deplored the abominably poor handwriting found among the English population. At present the head teacher at each school in England, according to the author, may decide whether cursive, script, or joined script will be taught. Hurdls suggested the need for national handwriting standards. He stated that such standards should require a return to the traditional, free-arm, round, cursive style of writing.

. . . and others say they can. Erlebacher and Herrick (10), working in Wisconsin, compared the quality of handwriting in 1959 with samples of script prevalent in 1912. Using Ayres' 1912 handwriting scale, the Wisconsin samples of handwriting were compared with those from the earlier era. Since students in the 1912 study were in the upper elementary school, samples of 677 sixth grade students were gathered in 20 Wisconsin schools for purposes of comparison.

Erlebacher and Herrick (10) concluded that (a) there is a strong indication that the 1912 and 1959 samples did not differ meaningfully in median legibility and (b) if the populations were representative, there is little reason to make the general claim that the handwriting of today's children has deteriorated. It should be pointed out that the conclusions were based on the findings of competent researchers and not on subjective opinion, as in the case of the Irwin and Hurdls articles.

Reviews of Research in Handwriting

Under the direction of Herrick, the Committee on Research in the Basic Skills completed its report, *Ten Years of Research in Handwriting, 1949-1959* (4). The research studies of the committee were organized in six major categories:

1. Surveys of Practice and Present Knowledge About Handwriting
2. Dimensions of the Handwriting Act
3. Pressure and Motor Behavior in Handwriting
4. Perception of the Normative and Aspirational Factors in Handwriting
5. Human Factors in the Design of Instruments for Handwriting
6. Factors in and Measurement of Legibility in Handwriting.

On the bases provided by a survey of related literature, questionnaires, laboratory tests, and random sampling techniques, the committee reported the results of a decade of research on handwriting and related factors. Among the findings were:

1. The regular classroom teacher usually taught writing.

2. Most programs included instruction in both manuscript and cursive writing. The shift from manuscript to cursive writing was usually made between grades two and four.

3. Seventy-three percent of schools surveyed began instruction in grade one; 88 percent by the end of grade two.

4. Three-fourths of the schools had instruction through grade six; one-half through grade eight.

5. Modal length for handwriting periods was fifteen minutes, usually five times a week.

6. Most teachers relied on commercially prepared materials.

7. The improvement and control of efficient motor patterns under the various conditions of handwriting depended more on the cognitive and perceptual processes than on the establishment of automatic behavior.

This was a thorough and intensive study of handwriting, and it was made widely available.

Herrick (21) also wrote an article in an effort to clarify the nature and function of handwriting in written language. This article discussed research studies done by other people and presented their findings. His 1960 report included the following statements:

1. There has been a trend toward simplicity in the formation of letters and numerals.

2. The letters *r, e,* and *a* are major troublemakers.

3. Two basic movements necessary for writing are: (a) inscriptive function and (b) cursive function.

4. The most efficient angle of pursuit lies between 135° and 160°.

5. Velocity of hand movement is modified by the size of a letter, combinations of the letters, the nature of the stroke being made, and the direction of the stroke.

6. Maturity in handwriting expresses itself in less and more even pressure.

7. Size, width, and angle of letters are closely related.

8. The time of writing does not vary, to a degree, with the length of stroke, the direction of stroke, or with the number of strokes.

9. Cursive writing is a little faster than manuscript up to the junior high school period.

10. The legibility of adult handwriting may be affected significantly by the extent to which handwriting is used, by the sex of the writer, and by the occupation held by the writer.

11. Left-handed children do not perform as well, in quality and speed, as do those using the right hand.

12. Preferred writing instruments were fountain pen, ball point pen, and adult pencil.

13. One can distinguish between two samples of handwriting as to legibility and recognize which is better.

14. No simple single factor of handwriting distinguishes between samples of good and bad handwriting alone.

DeBoer (6), in 1961, published in the *Review of Educational Research* a brief report on some studies not included by Herrick in 1960. These included the Freeman (1958) and Foster (1957) studies on cursive and manuscript writing; the Harris and Rarick (1957) study on pressure and legibility; the Enstrom (1957) report on handedness; the Quint (1958) study on aversion to handwriting; Seifert's (1959) paper on the personal handwriting of children in grades six through nine; the Templin (1959) and Hildreth (1960) reports and summaries on legibility; and the Harris and Herrick (1959) studies of middle grade children's judgment of handwriting. Several of these studies will be described in greater detail in other sections of this monograph.

Surveys of handwriting practices in different states as well as handwriting instruments, speed and quality, and teaching and learning were discussed by Harris (16) in the *Encyclopedia of Educational Research*. Among the findings reported are these:

1. Copying in learning handwriting has long been established as a method preferable to tracing.

2. There is evidence that copying ability in children from six to nine years of age is itself a variable which develops rapidly until about age seven and more slowly thereafter.

3. An approach to the assaying of legibility of handwriting is that of determining the specific letter forms that account for most of the illegibilities in writing. These letters appear to be *a, e, n, t*. This suggests that preventive work and corrective work in handwriting instruction could be formulated quite specifically to concentrate on particular illegibilities in handwriting.

4. With respect to special disabilities, in the areas of agraphia, mirror writing, and so-called writer's cramp, extensive research has been conducted.

5. From recent conclusions, the rate and success of sinistrals (left-handed persons) in handwriting appear more closely related to techniques used in writing with the left hand than to hand preference.

6. Children of different ability levels may differ significantly in their perception of the handwriting task and in their ability to appraise their own handwriting as a basis for further improvement.

Manuscript and Cursive Writing

For many years teachers and parents have debated the relative merits of manuscript and cursive writing in the elementary schools. Although schools have varied in regard to practices in handwriting instruction, most children today learn both forms of writing. However, some people feel that teaching two systems is confusing to a large number of children, and as such, support the view that schools should teach only manuscript *or* only cursive. Other persons enthusiastically endorse the teaching of "italic" handwriting. Each group stresses the qualities of excellence that their program supposedly promotes. As a result, questions continue to center around what style or styles of handwriting should be taught, which style is the most rapid and legible, and when the transition to cursive should occur if manuscript writing is taught to young children.

Some say "yea" and some say "nay." Foster (12), Leavitt and Johnson (32), Herrick (22), and Hildreth (27) have concerned themselves with separate studies and surveys of the literature regarding the present state of educational thought and research concerning manuscript and cursive writing. Foster (12) in 1957 investigated children's handwriting in grades three through six in public schools in which manuscript was taught in the early grades, and the change to cursive writing occurred in grade six. He concluded:

1. Manuscript writing is only slightly more legible than is cursive.

2. Children who write one style legibly also tend to write the other style legibly.

3. If the writing is legible, the style is immaterial, and, conversely, both styles are highly illegible if poorly written.

4. In general, children who have been taught handwriting in the public schools write cursive style faster than they do manuscript.

5. From grade three through grade six, there is a consistent increase in the speed of writing both styles of handwriting.

6. After it is introduced into the program, the speed of writing cursive rapidly begins to equal and then to surpass that of the manuscript style.

Leavitt and Johnson (32) summarized selected studies from 1926 to 1956 that were concerned with the merits and disadvantages of both cursive and manuscript writing. They concluded that (a) there is a tendency to develop procedures in the teaching of handwriting that harmonize with the child's physical, mental, and emotional growth; (b) manuscript writing is used in the large majority of schools; (c) from the point of view of speed, quality, expression, spelling, and reading, manuscript writing should be taught and used in the primary grades; and (d) present data tend to indicate that cursive writing is superior after grade three, but more study is needed to support this viewpoint fully.

Herrick (22) wrote a paper in which he presented comparative data on manuscript and cursive writing. According to this article, the arguments for using manuscript writing rest on three propositions: (a) the straight line, circle, and spacing forms of manuscript are more in line with the motor and eye-hand-arm coordination of young children than are the complex movements and letter formations of the cursive system; (b) manuscript writing resembles the printed symbols the child is learning to read and thus he does not have to learn to read two forms of written language at the same time; and (c) manuscript writing is generally more legible than cursive. Herrick also cited the four main points which often are made by the proponents of cursive writing: (a) cursive writing is the more socially accepted form of handwriting; (b) manuscript writing is slower and more tension producing; (c) the manuscript signature is not legal; and (d) manuscript writing lacks individuality and character. Herrick also discusses the transition from manuscript to cursive writing and presents many helpful suggestions for teachers to employ in helping children develop their handwriting skill to their appropriate level of quality and efficiency.

In 1960 Hildreth (27) reviewed expert opinion and research conducted by authorities in the field of education and concluded:

1. There is no significant difference in rate between the styles of writing (cursive and manuscript) when experience and practice are comparable for upper grade students.

2. Rate of handwriting is more closely allied to quality of instruction, duration of practice, and traits of the writer than to the particular style of handwriting.

3. Fluency in handwriting, just as in reading and other skills, is an indication of high automatization of the skill.

4. One essential difference between manuscript and cursive writing is that, as the child matures, with a speeded up rate of handwriting, superior legibility can be observed.

5. There is a need to develop norms for rate and quality of manuscript writing throughout the elementary grades. At present, there are no such norms for manuscript writing. There are norms for cursive writing within the elementary grades.

All in all, it would seem that on the basis of both current practice and research findings concerned with the teaching of manuscript and cursive writing, it would be prudent to agree with Herrick (22) when he states that today changes in writing styles do not shake our educational and social foundations and do not merit the excitement they create.

You don't have to agree with either group. In 1959 in the Catlin Gable School of Portland, Oregon, Berry (3) conducted a study which suggested that italic writing was a superior form to either cursive or manuscript as a form of writing. Students were given special handwriting instruction in italic writing, with pupils in grades one through five using it exclusively, while students in grades six through eight used it on a voluntary basis. Berry reported that papers improved in legibility and appearance and that students were enthusiastic and considered it a privilege to be a part of an experimental group. She further stated that italic writing was practical, sensible, and basic to both cursive and manuscript writing. She also reported that italic handwriting had been used so successfully in English schools for the past ten years that the use of it was no longer considered an experimental venture.

Why do schools change from manuscript to cursive? Groff (15) during 1959 sent questionnaires to the directors of elementary education in 72 of the more populous metropolitan areas in the United States. He asked them to check any of 20 reasons why they changed from manuscript to cursive writing at certain grade levels and provided space for them to comment. Social systems evidently changed because of tradition and wide current practice rather than on the basis of research findings. The directors felt that the change from manuscript to cursive writing also encouraged faster writing.

If you change, when should you change? Freeman (14), long an authority in the field of handwriting, has supplied information which should be of interest to persons concerned with the time when the change from manuscript to cursive writing is most commonly made and the reasons for the timing of the change. Questionnaires were sent to 1,294 cities in the United States with a population of 10,000 and over. The number of replies returned was 861, or 66 percent.

The findings and conclusions were:

1. The prevailing practice in the cities of the United States of 10,000 and above is to make the change in grade three. The number of school systems in which the change is made in the third grade, of those who reported, is 570 as against 355 cities which make the change in grade two.

2. There is considerable variation in practice among the states, which may be attributed largely to a difference in practice encouraged by the writing systems used.

3. Authorities differ as to the time for making the changeover, though the majority favor the change in grade three.

4. The theoretical considerations cited as reasons for making the change in one or the other grade strongly favor grade three by a vote of 372 against 174.

5. Pending more objective scientific investigation, which may be difficult, the weight of evidence seems to be in favor of changing from manuscript to cursive in grade three.

6. Any program should be flexible enough to allow for some individual variation in making the change.

In addition to this study, Freeman (13) in 1960 reported his endeavor to collect and rate specimens for a handwriting scale. A total of 162 cities in 43 states agreed to cooperate. The number of schools represented in each grade varied from 127 to 216; the number of pupils, from 10,646 to 22,374. In its final form, the scale consisted of five specimens of handwriting for each grade. The specimens were selected from a total of 135,491 samples representing children's handwriting throughout the country. For grades one and two, the scale is in manuscript writing; for grades three through eight, the scale is in cursive writing.

Enstrom (8) also discussed when cursive writing should be introduced, based on his experience in working with teachers and as a director of the teaching of cursive writing in many schools. He felt that instruction in cursive writing should begin when the children are ready and that this would usually be before the middle of the second grade. This viewpoint differs from the findings reported by Freeman (14), both in terms of prevailing practice and the views of a number of other authorities regarding the optimum time for change.

Pressure and Handwriting

Harris and Rarick (17; 18) have completed several studies on pressure and handwriting. In 1957 they reported on their examination of handwriting pressure patterns manifested at varied rates of writing with particular reference to the interrelationships among point pressure, legibility of handwriting, rate of writing, and motor control. Individual and group techniques of analysis were used. Three studies were made. The first two were exploratory studies which were helpful in shaping the general design of the third study. The population for the third study consisted of ten students whose handwriting had been judged easy to read and nine students whose handwriting had been judged difficult to read. Handwriting samples were selected from the final examination papers of 230 undergraduate students in educational psychology at the University of Wisconsin. Each student selected to participate in the study was tested individually. The raw data consisted of three writing samples, three pressure records, and the results of a motor control test. Among the findings of this study were the points that:

1. Fast writing was associated with higher pressure, greater force variability, and poorer legibility.

2. The average amount of pressure exerted in handwriting is a highly individual matter. The use of handwriting drills designed to develop a uniform level of point pressure in all pupils is highly questionable.

3. The speed of writing is a relative and highly individual matter. If a student is forced to write faster than his usual comfortable rate, the legibility of handwriting will almost certainly deteriorate.

4. Most legible handwriting will be provided by those pupils with the greatest degree of fine motor control of the hand.

5. Great variations in legibility may be expected in children.

In 1959 Harris and Rarick (18) continued their investigation of point pressure and legibility in regard to the handwriting of boys and girls in the elementary school. Since their previous study with college students had indicated that high legibility tends to be accompanied by relatively low variability in point force while low legibility tends to be accompanied by relatively high variability in point force, they wanted to examine the relationships between these two factors with younger students. The subjects included 144 boys and girls selected at random from grades four, six, and ten. All students were right-handed, had continuous experience in a given school system, and were within the normal age range for their grade. Here again the subjects were tested individually, and pressures and times were electrically recorded. The following findings were reported:

1. Sex and grade differences were present but could not be identified with differences in point pressure.

2. When subjects moved away from their normal writing tempo, high legibility tended to be associated with low variability of application of force and vice versa.

3. If speed of handwriting is increased, variability in application of force is likewise increased, the motor set is disturbed, and writing legibility is adversely affected.

Two years later Herrick and Otto (24) conducted further investigations and extended the research in pressure. In this study, primarily exploratory, they attempted to (a) examine grip pressure applied to the barrel of a writing instrument by electronic means and (b) examine patterns and relationships that would facilitate the identification of pertinent questions for further study. Their overall conclusion was that while handwriting appears to be a highly personalized act, certain group tendencies can be identified in pressure phenomena. They also pointed out implications for further study.

Right Hand or Left Hand?

Teachers' interest in the effects of changes in handedness both on speech patterns and on children's social and emotional development continues to remain high. Because the experts themselves continue to disagree about these effects, most schools, in general practice, permit the child to use the hand which he prefers. For the most part, teachers help children make whatever adjustments are needed regardless of their hand dominance. Several persons have contributed further knowledge to assist us in the teaching of handwriting.

Enstrom's (9) doctoral dissertation reports that, in response to a questionnaire sent to 10,000 teachers in Pennsylvania and Ohio and a few schools in New York and New Jersey, 11.14 percent of 92,656 pupils surveyed were found to be writing with their left hands. Of this group, 12.5 percent were boys and 9.7 percent were girls. He stated that, contrary to previous reports, rate and success in handwriting with the left hand, for this group of children, were more closely related to the technique used than to the hand preferred. He also presented findings based on a study of 1,103 children which suggest those approaches holding the greatest promise of success for teaching left-handed writers.

Trankell (47) closely followed the writing habits of more than 700 left-handed children from the first through the fourth grade in the elementary schools of Stockholm from 1949 to 1953. She was particularly interested in the extent to which the left-handers' choice of writing hand influenced the quality and speed of handwriting. She stated:

1. Left-handed children who write with the same hand all through their school life achieve on an average a better handwriting than those left-handers, who for a longer or shorter time, write with the hand that is not ultimately going to be their writing hand.

2. No statistically significant difference was found between the quality of the handwriting of the consistent left-handed writers and the left-handers who consistently use their right hand for writing.

3. There is no safe ground for assuming that the consistent left-handed writers will have more difficulty in achieving a good handwriting than right-handers of the same sex and intelligence.

4. No difference was found between the quality of the handwriting of left-handers who spontaneously chose their right hand for writing and right-handers of the same sex and intelligence.

5. Left-handers, who practiced right-handed writing under compulsion, either self-imposed or applied from the outside, have a somewhat smaller chance to achieve a good quality of the handwriting than have the right-handers.

6. The strength of the left-hand tendencies plays a decisive part in the choice of writing hand and the development of the writing habits.

7. The best way to help the left-handed child in his choice of writing hand is to make as perfect a diagnosis as possible of the nature and strength of his left-hand tendencies. By increasing the chance to make a correct primary choice of writing hand, the possibility to reach a good handwriting will also be increased.

In England, Smith and Reed (40) investigated the relative speed of left- and right-handed children by studying 140 children (70 girls and 70 boys), ages 8 to 14, drawn from six schools. Seventy of the children were right-handed and seventy of them were left-handed. The researchers concluded:

1. While the results showed a tendency for the right-handed groups to write more rapidly than left-handed, when both sets of children used the preferred hand, the difference in writing speeds is not statistically significant.

2. Findings indicated a relatively higher degree of skill for the non-preferred hands of the left-handed children.

3. Environmental factors played a greater part than neural differences with their associated muscular, perceptual, and mechanical difficulties.

General Advice

While teachers can glean helpful information from all articles mentioned in this chapter, some studies seem to fall most appropriately under a general section, and as such, are included in the paragraphs which follow.

Personal styles of handwriting. Seifert (38) analyzed and classified the styles of personal handwriting among pupils in grades six, seven, eight, and nine by obtaining five separate handwriting samples from 1,020 pupils. She found that at least one-third of the population at each grade level showed evidence of using a personal style of handwriting although the findings were inconclusive as to when pupils started to use this personal style. The quality of the handwriting was generally good and more than half of the youngsters in the population studied stated that they found their personal style quicker and easier to use, while one-third found this more attractive than other types.

Improving handwriting skills. Wagner (48) prepared an interesting report on an improvement program in handwriting in operation in the New York City schools. The report included not only a description of the improvement program but a follow-up of improvement studies and a diagnostic chart for cursive writing. Headley (19), following a study of children in the kindergartens in Minneapolis, Minnesota, suggested ways in which children during this year can prepare for writing experiences in later years. He stated that writing as a drill skill should not be introduced in kindergarten. However, children should have opportunities:

1. To develop muscle and eye-hand coordination
2. To appreciate the left to right sequence in words
3. To appreciate the fact that letters are placed on a horizontal base line
4. To be alerted to the fact that there are several kinds of letter symbols which may be used in writing
5. To see how manuscript letters are formed.

Quint (34) was concerned with the problems of children's aversion to handwriting and the respective relationships between this aversion and intelligence, motor ability, personality, and achievement in handwriting, spelling, and written recall. After examining 626 sixth grade children, she reported:

1. Left-handed children show the same attitude toward handwriting as do right-handed children.
2. Change of handedness does not affect attitude toward writing.
3. Children who disliked handwriting find their writing unsatisfactory in spite of real effort.

56

4. Children disliking handwriting find formation of letters the most difficult aspect.

5. Seventy-two percent prefer writing on their own to writing in penmanship class.

6. If sixth grade children could do as they like in penmanship class, they would practice only those things that give them trouble.

7. Children who disliked handwriting were poorer writers when writing was done with a pencil and showed greater difficulties in letter size, spacing, slant, alignment, and line quality. They had significantly lower scores in motor ability and in personality tests.

Warrender (49) pointed out problems of handwriting at the sixth grade level and suggested steps the teacher should follow in improving children's writing skills.

Commercial systems of handwriting. Herrick (20) prepared an interesting and comprehensive report on the different commercial systems of handwriting now available in the United States. In his report, he describes what present commercial system practices are like and contrasts them with respect to points of concern to teachers. The report does not attempt to evaluate these practices; rather it is intended to inform teachers and administrators about comparative commercial practices in handwriting. Herrick and Otto (23) supplemented the previously mentioned bulletin with another report which was devoted to a comparison of the various letter form models recommended by the commercial handwriting systems.

Summary

Most educators seem in agreement that handwriting is no longer an art but a necessary tool. It is also more than a tool in that it is a means through which the individual may express himself in a highly personalized manner. Most persons would agree that while there are various adequate systems of teaching handwriting, the important role that the teacher must assume is that of adjusting instructional procedures to the developmental pattern of the individual learner.

Legibility, ease, and simplicity of writing, as well as comfort and economy of time are prime considerations in the teaching of handwriting. These—rather than systematic, formal, and ritualistic attempts to have children exactly imitate models—are the factors which will contribute most to the child's feeling of achievement.

Bibliography

1. ALVA, CHARLES. "Structure Grammar in California Schools." *English Journal* 49:606-11; December 1960.

2. BATEMAN, DONALD R. "More Mature Writing Through a Better Understanding of Language Structure." *English Journal* 50:457-60, 468; October 1961.

3. BERRY, WINIFRED. "Italic Writing." *Education Digest* 26:50-51; April 1961.

4. COMMITTEE ON RESEARCH IN BASIC SKILLS. *Ten Years of Research in Handwriting, 1949-1959.* Madison: Department of Education, University of Wisconsin. 26 p. Mimeographed.

5. CRAWFORD, KATHERINE, and NEAL R. EDMUND. "Letter-Writing Ability of Fourth Grade Pupils." *Peabody Journal of Education* 39:28-30; July 1961.

6. DEBOER, JOHN J. "Composition, Handwriting, and Spelling: Teaching of Handwriting." *Review of Educational Research* 31:166-67; April 1961.

7. DEBOER, JOHN J. "Grammar in Language Teaching." *Elementary English* 36:413-21; October 1959.

8. ENSTROM, ERIC ALFRED. "After Manuscript Writing, When Shall We Begin Cursive?" *Elementary School Journal* 61:24-27; October 1960.

9. ENSTROM, ERIC ALFRED. "The Extent of the Use of the Left Hand in Handwriting and the Determination of the Relative Efficiency of the Various Hand-Wrist-Arm-Paper Adjustments." *Dissertation Abstracts* 17:1036-37; No. 5; 1957.

10. ERLEBACHER, ADRIENNE, and VIRGIL E. HERRICK. "Quality of Handwriting Today and Yesterday." *Elementary School Journal,* Vol. 62, No. 2. Chicago: University of Chicago Press with the Department of Education of the University of Chicago, 1961. p. 89-93.

11. FORD, PAUL M. "Lay Readers in the High School Composition Program: Some Statistics." *English Journal* 50:522-28; November 1961.

12. FOSTER, EMMET A. "A Comparison of Intermediate Grade Manuscript and Cursive Handwriting in Two Typical Elementary School Programs." *Dissertation Abstracts* 17:2934-35; No. 12; 1957.

13. FREEMAN, FRANK N. "New Handwriting Scale." *Elementary School Journal* 59:218-21; January 1959.

14. FREEMAN, FRANK N. "Transition from Manuscript to Cursive." *Elementary English* 35:366-72; October 1958.

15. GROFF, P. J. "From Manuscript to Cursive, Why?" *Elementary School Journal* 61:97-101; November 1960.

16. HARRIS, THEODORE L. "Handwriting." *Encyclopedia of Educational Research.* Chester W. Harris, editor. Third edition. New York: The Macmillan Company, 1960. p. 616-24.

17. HARRIS, THEODORE L., and G. L. RARICK. "Problem of Pressure in Handwriting." *Journal of Experimental Education* 26:151-78; December 1957.

18. HARRIS, THEODORE L., and G. L. RARICK. "Relationship Between Handwriting Pressure and Legibility of Handwriting in Children and Adolescents." *Journal of Experimental Education* 28:65-84; September 1959.

19. HEADLEY, N. "To Write or Not To Write." *Childhood Education* 37:260-63; February 1961.

20. HERRICK, VIRGIL E. *Comparison of Practices in Handwriting Advocated by Nineteen Commercial Systems of Handwriting Instruction.* Madison: Committee on Research in Basic Skills, University of Wisconsin, July 1960.

21. HERRICK, VIRGIL E. "Handwriting and Children's Writing." *Elementary English* 37:264-67; February 1961.

22. HERRICK, VIRGIL E. "Manuscript and Cursive Writing." *Childhood Education* 37:264-67; February 1961.

23. HERRICK, VIRGIL E., and WAYNE OTTO. *Letter Form Models Advocated by Commercial Handwriting Systems.* Madison: School of Education, University of Wisconsin, 1961. 25 p.

24. HERRICK, VIRGIL E., and WAYNE OTTO. "Pressure on Point and Barrel of a Writing Instrument." *Journal of Experimental Education* 30:215-30; No. 2; December 1961.

25. HEYS, FRANK, JR. "A Theme a Week?" *English Leaflet* 59:28-31; Fall 1960.

26. HEYS, FRANK, JR. *Report of Experiment in Teaching Composition.* Massachusetts: Department of English, Lincoln-Sudbury Regional High School. 10 p. Mimeographed.

27. HILDRETH, G. "Manuscript Writing After Sixty Years." *Elementary English* 37:3-13; January 1960.

28. HURDLS, V. "Standard of Writing." *London Times Educational Supplement* 2368:439; October 7, 1960.

29. IRWIN, T. "Why Our Kids Can't Write." *Saturday Evening Post,* September 10, 1955. p. 122-24.

30. KING, FRED M. "Handwriting Practices in Our Schools Today." *Elementary English* 38:483-86, 493; November 1961.

31. LAMAR, WILMET A., compiler. "Freshman Composition Courses in Ten Illinois Colleges." *Illinois English Bulletin* 48:1-19; December 1960.

32. LEAVITT, JEROME E., and HAZEL S. JOHNSON. "Handwriting." *Curriculum Bulletin,* Vol. 9, No. 124. Eugene: University of Oregon, January 1956. 12 p. Mimeographed.

33. MERSAND, JOSEPH. "What Has Happened to Written Composition?" *English Journal* 50:231-37; April 1961.

34. QUINT, GERALDINE H. "Aversions to Handwriting." *Dissertation Abstracts* 19:2031; No. 8; 1959.

35. REMONDINO, C. "Factorial Analysis of the Evaluation of Scholastic Composition in the Mother Tongue." *British Journal of Educational Psychology* 29:242-51; November 1959.

36. ROBINSON, NORA. "The Relation Between Knowledge of English Grammar and Ability in English Composition." *British Journal of Educational Psychology* 30: 184-86; Part II; June 1960.

37. SCHAICK, SALLY. "The Composition Reading Machine." *English Journal* 29:237-41; April 1960.

38. SEIFERT, ELIS PATRICIA. "Personal Styles of Handwriting in Grades Six, Seven, Eight, and Nine." *Dissertation Abstracts* 20:3581; No. 20; 1960.

39. SISTER ELISE MARIE. "Developing a Writing Unit." *Catholic Educational Review* 59:83-90; February 1961.

40. SMITH, A. C., and G. F. REED. "Experimental Investigation of the Relative Speeds of Left- and Right-Handed Writers." *Journal of Genetic Psychology* 94:67-76; March 1959.

41. STRICKLAND, RUTH G. "Evaluating Children's Composition." *Elementary English* 39:321-31; May 1960.

42. STROM, INGRID M. "Do Grammar Drills Help Writing Skills?" *NEA Journal* 49:25; December 1960.

43. STROM, INGRID M. "Research in Grammar and Usage and Its Implications for Teaching Writing." *Bulletin of the School of Education,* Vol. 36, No. 5. Bloomington: Indiana University, September 1960. 23 p.

44. STROM, INGRID M. "Research in Teaching Grammar and Usage." *Education Digest* 26:50-52; January 1961.

45. Suggs, Lena Reddick. "Structural Grammar Versus Traditional Grammar in Influencing Writing." *English Journal* 50:174-78; March 1961.

46. Templin, E. M. "How Important Is Handwriting Today?" *Elementary School Journal* 61:158-64; December 1960.

47. Trankell, A. "Influence of the Choice of Writing Hand on the Handwriting." *British Journal of Educational Psychology* 26:94-103; June 1956.

48. Wagner, Rosemary E. "Writing Is for Reading." *NEA Journal* 45:555-57; December 1956.

49. Warrender, G. "Penmanship." *Grade Teacher* 78:50; January 1961.

50. Zeigler, Martin L., and Lewis M. Herman. "A Study of the Effectiveness of a Summer Remedial Course in English for College Freshmen." *Journal of Educational Research* 53:76-78; October 1959.

Chapter Four

Written Expression

AS REPORTED in the 1955 *Research Helps in Teaching the Language Arts,* there was little or no research specifically devoted to creative written expression. The passing years have not appreciably changed the situation. There is literature available which hopefully presents viewpoints and techniques for helping children learn to write creatively, but there is little if any basic research to substantiate these positions with evidence. As a result, this brief chapter reviews some of the current opinions as to creative writing and also reviews some of the literature directed toward improving written expression in general.

Teachers' Queries

While teachers asked some questions about creative writing, there were fewer questions asked about this topic than about others. For the main part, teachers evidenced concern over: (a) What is meant by *creative writing?* (b) *Can* creative writing be taught, and if so, *how* can it be taught? and (c) How can we help children achieve skill in written communication whether it be classified as creative expression or not? The answers to these questions, in the light of the literature available, are discussed in this chapter.

Some Statements About Creativity

Peterson and Robinson (48) discussed aspects and implications of creativity. In their article they first examined various definitions given to the term "creativity." They then investigated methods used in studying the creative process by analyzing research methods. In addition, they described the creative process and factors in creativity as well as their educational implications and unsolved problems in the area of creativity. Concerned with the *process* of creative writing, McEnroe (44) described the results of her work with sixth grade children. The *values* of creative writing were

61

presented by Witty (68), who also defined and illustrated what he deemed to be creative writing and attempted to stimulate thinking as to ways of generating such writing.

Can Creative Writing Be Taught?

In 1958, Cahill (9; 8) published two papers which emphasized his points that creativity cannot really be taught and that the teacher can only serve as a catalyst by giving the child the tools, interest, hope, and excitement needed to do this kind of writing. General statements about creative writing and its role in helping children better express their interests, problems, and ideas have been prepared by Hughes (30), Crossley (12), and LaBrant (37) in articles designed for teachers desirous of developing this type of writing. A dissenting vote against the theory that the main purpose of an English teacher was to teach creativity was expressed by Withers (66). He felt that exposition as a form of writing was necessary for all children, but "creative writing" was a luxury most high school students could not afford.

Suggestions for Helping Children with Creative Writing

Several writers have contributed thoughtful suggestions with respect to helping children to write. Strickland (61), in her book, *Language Arts in the Elementary School,* provides many pertinent observations concerning the teaching of written language. Teachers will profit from reading the entire section on this topic. Many teachers undoubtedly would agree with the following points made by Hughes (31): (a) learning to write is a long, complex process; (b) the increased ability to use language is partially dependent upon the psychological maturation of the individual; and (c) all writing must be meaningful to the writer.

Additional recommendations, made by other writers, are summarized under the subheadings which follow:

General recommendations. After comparing different methods used in helping children write creatively, Wagner (65) briefly and specifically presented the findings of her study as they reflected practices on the national scene in metropolitan areas. Kennedy (33) described how she fostered creative writing by preparing a highly adventurous story developed around characters who were members of her class. Witty and Martin (69) reported on their study which dealt with the potentiality of a silent film in building both interest and motivation for creative expression.

Another interesting approach, in which current periodicals were used, was presented by Robinson (52). Emphasizing the fact that nine-tenths of what is taught in social studies involves some form of the language arts, Applegate (1) urged that, in many instances, the two can be combined easily and naturally. In turn, Blum (5) contended that the core type of program lends itself readily to personalized reading and writing programs.

Two papers of particular interest to teachers whose main work is with young children were written by Pounds and Mattila. Pounds (49) suggested methods for stimulating preschoolers' interest in writing and Mattila (43) explained ways in which teachers in the primary grades may guide the young child's development of expressive skills. Three publications were specifically concerned with writing at the fourth grade level. They were published by Lorence (40), Reeves (50), and Mattera (42). Larom (39) described a program he developed with sixth graders in Montana during the fall of 1959. For suggestions on evaluating children's creative expression, the reader is referred to materials written by Green (23) in 1957.

Direct experiences and creative writing. Edmund became interested in the extent to which intermediate grade pupils drew on their personal problems, fears, and worries as topics for written compositions in school. In addition, his writing reflected interest in the relationship between prior experiences and the creative quality of stories written by this age student.

Edmund has written many articles, as noted in the bibliography (17; 20; 18; 16; 15; 13; and 14). He also (19) draws together limited reports of research in writing and raises questions which suggest the need for better research designs. He stated that the literature reveals that most of the investigations in writing tend to group themselves around the following major topics: (a) writing as a way of identifying and motivating gifted children; (b) experiences forming the bases for children's stories; (c) pupil interest as related to the selection of writing topics; (d) methods and materials appropriate for teaching writing; and (e) writing and total personal involvement.

Written Expression: General Statements

New approaches to writing have been discussed in recent "broad overview" articles. Among these, plans for grouping for instruction to provide for individual differences have been explored, as have ways of managing students' writing assignments. Also, the importance of writing as a tool of communication has been reviewed. The reader is referred to statements of LaBrant (36), Roody (53), Gregory (24), Kraus (35), Sparks (58), Brother Edward Patrick (6), Cherniss (10), Beggs (4), and Wittick (67) regarding these points.

Several studies have been completed which are quite specific with respect to ways of fostering good written expression. Monk's (46) efforts were concerned with assessing the relationship between children's home environment and their school achievement in written English. Some writers have delved into ways of encouraging children to write more effective compositions, and to this end, sentence structure, spelling, usage, content, clarity, and other related topics have been examined. The writings of Peck (47), Sister Mary L. Moe (57), Grubbs (26), Keene (32), Crawford and Edmund (11), Barbe (2), Loughlin (41), Kraus (34), Stensland (59), and Rosenson (54) cast light upon these matters.

Evaluation procedures. Ellis (21) reported on his study involving the evaluation of the overall effectiveness of the written language program in grades four and six in the San Diego City schools, while Heed (27) discussed his work in Vermont in determining whether children really do grow in their ability to write compositions.

A plan for having greater student participation in checking and evaluating compositions was proposed by Grissom (25). Stressing the need for evaluation of written composition so that the child may be aware of his progress and continue to grow, Strickland (60) suggested concrete ways in which both teacher-evaluation and self-evaluation by the pupil can motivate the learner to progress along an educational continuum.

Summary

Interest in creative writing continues to be high, but definite research in the area remains at low ebb. On the basis of the literature available, however, the classroom teacher should obtain many fine *subjective* suggestions for more effective instruction in written language. Some teachers may care to study the work of men like Torrance (64), Getzels and Jackson (22), and Bruner (7) to increase their understanding of creativity, in general, and its role in the educational process.

Bibliography

1. APPLEGATE, MAUREE. "We Must Clear the Landscape To Get at the Soil." *Grade Teacher* 75:38; January 1958.
2. BARBE, RICHARD H. *An Estimation and Examination of the Structural Element of Prose Writing.* Columbus: The Ohio State University, 1961.
3. BATEMAN, DONALD R. "More Mature Writing Through a Better Understanding of Language Structure." *English Journal* 50:457-60, 468; October 1961.
4. BEGGS, BERENICE. "They Learn To Write by Writing." *English Journal* 44:292-93; May 1955.
5. BLUM, MARTIN. " 'Personal' Reading and Writing." *English Journal* 44:36-37; January 1955.

6. BROTHER EDWARD PATRICK, F.S.C. "High School Achievement in English." *Clearing House* 35:301-302; January 1961.

7. BRUNER, JEROME S. *On Knowing; Essays for the Left Hand.* Cambridge, Massachusetts: Belknap Press of Harvard University, 1962. 165 p.

8. CAHILL, WALTER T. "Can You *Teach* Creative Writing?" *Clearing House* 33:165-66; November 1958.

9. CAHILL, WALTER T. "Writing for Real." *Clearing House* 32:304-305; January 1958.

10. CHERNISS, IRVIN R. "The Art of Composition: A New Approach." *High Points* 37:36-43; April 1955.

11. CRAWFORD, KATHERINE, and NEAL R. EDMUND. "Letter-Writing Ability of Fourth Grade Pupils." *Peabody Journal of Education* 39:28-30; July 1961.

12. CROSSLEY, ALICE B. "Can We Help Children To Write?" *Journal of Education* 139:13-19; February 1957.

13. EDMUND, NEAL R. "Do Fifth Grade Pupils Write Stories Based on Personal Interests?" *Peabody Journal of Education* 36:151-58; November 1958.

14. EDMUND, NEAL R. "Do Intermediate Grade Pupils Write About Their Problems?" *Elementary English* 37:242-43; April 1960.

15. EDMUND, NEAL R. "Quality of Creative Writing Based on Direct Experiences." *Clearing House* 33:163-64; November 1958.

16. EDMUND, NEAL R. "Relationship Between Prior Experiences and the Creative Quality of Stories." *Elementary English* 35:248-49; April 1958.

17. EDMUND, NEAL R. "Story Writing in the Seventh Grade." *Elementary English* 34:305-306; May 1957.

18. EDMUND, NEAL R. "A Study of the Relationship Between Prior Experiences and the Quality of Creative Writing Done by Seventh-Grade Pupils." *Journal of Educational Research* 51:481-92; March 1958.

19. EDMUND, NEAL R. "Writing in the Intermediate Grades." *Elementary English* 36:491-501; November 1959.

20. EDUCATIONAL NEWS AND EDITORIAL COMMENT. "What Seventh Graders Write About." *Elementary School Journal* 58:129; December 1957.

21. ELLIS, GEORGE M. "An Evaluation of a Written Language Program." *Research Relating to Children.* Bulletin No. 11. Children's Bureau, U.S. Department of Health, Education, and Welfare. Washington, D.C.: Superintendent of Documents, Government Printing Office, 1960. p. 68-69.

22. GETZELS, JACOB W., and PHILIP W. JACKSON. *Creativity and Intelligence; Explorations with Gifted Students.* New York: John Wiley & Sons, Inc., 1962. 293 p.

23. GREEN, A. S. "Evaluating Creative, Expressive Writing." *American Childhood* 43:45; November 1957.

24. GREGORY, EMILY B. "Managing Student Writing." *English Journal* 44:18-25; January 1955.

25. GRISSOM, LOREN V. "Student Leadership in Evaluating Composition." *English Journal* 48:338-39; September 1959.

26. GRUBBS, B. "Putting English into Practice." *Elementary English* 38:292-97; May 1961.

27. HEED, HELEN. "Children Certainly Do Improve Their Writing Skills." *Clearing House* 30:365-68; February 1956.

28. HEYS, FRANK, JR. *Report of Experiment in Teaching Composition.* Massachusetts: Department of English, Lincoln-Sudbury Regional High School. 10 p. Mimeographed.

29. HEYS, FRANK, JR. "A Theme a Week?" *English Leaflet* 59:28-31; Fall 1960.
30. HUGHES, L. "Education for Creativity." *Overview* 2:38-39; July 1961.
31. HUGHES, MARIE M. "Writing: Too Early and Too Little." *Education* 76:463-67; April 1956
32. KEENE, KATHERINE. "Students Like Corrections." *English Journal* 45:212-15; April 1956.
33. KENNEDY, D. "Technique That Fostered Creative Writing." *Elementary English* 35:163-64; March 1958.
34. KRAUS, SILVY. "A Comparison of Three Methods of Teaching Sentence Structure." *English Journal* 46:276-81; May 1957.
35. KRAUS, SILVY. "Grouping for the Teaching of Composition." *English Journal* 48:402-404; October 1959.
36. LABRANT, L. L. "Inducing Students To Write." *English Journal* 44:70-74; February 1955.
37. LABRANT, L. L. "Writing—Most Difficult of Language Arts." *NEA Journal* 47:189-90; March 1958.
38. LAMAR, WILMER A., compiler. "Freshman Composition Courses in Ten Illinois Colleges." *Illinois English Bulletin* 48:1-19; December 1960.
39. LAROM, H. V. "Sixth Graders Write Good Short Stories." *Elementary English* 37:20-23; January 1960.
40. LORENCE, MARY C. "Small but Mighty Pens." *Grade Teacher* 75:30; January 1958.
41. LOUGHLIN, RICHARD L. "Think Before You Ink." *High Points* 37:16-27; February 1955.
42. MATTERA, GLORIA. "Authors, Fourth Grade Style." *Elementary English* 33:354-56; October 1956.
43. MATTILA, R. H. "Helping the Child on His Own in Writing" *Elementary English* 35:230-33; April 1958.
44. McENROE, KATHLEEN. "The Process of Creative Writing." *Elementary English* 35:159-62; March 1958.
45. MERSAND, JOSEPH. "What Has Happened to Written Composition?" *English Journal* 50:231-37; April 1961.
46. MONK, RICHARD J. "A Study To Determine the Relationship Between Children's Home Environments and Their School Achievement in Written English." *Dissertation Abstracts* 19:1619; No. 7; 1959. 230 p.
47. PECK, L. E. "Encouraging Written Expression in the Third Grade." *Instructor* 65:1; May 1956.
48. PETERSON, O. L., and J. T. ROBINSON. "Creativity: Some Aspects and Implications; Bibliography." *Science Education* 43:420-27; December 1959.
49. POUNDS, E. T. "How To Encourage Writing." *Parents Magazine* 32:46-47; February 1957.
50. REEVES, KATHERINE. "Gifts from the Fourth Grade." *Grade Teacher* 76:8; December 1958.
51. REMONDINO, C. "Factorial Analysis of the Evaluation of Scholastic Compositions in the Mother Tongue." *British Journal of Educational Psychology* 29:242-51; November 1959.
52. ROBINSON, MARJORIE C. "Around Again with Willie." *English Journal* 46:257-61; May 1957.
53. ROODY, SARAH I., and BESS LYMAN. "Managing Student Writing." *English Journal* 44:76-79; February 1955.
54. ROSENSON, J. S. "Oral Approach to Sentence Sense." *English Journal* 47:425-30; October 1958.

55. SCHUSTER, EDGAR H. "How Good Is the New Grammar?" *English Journal* 50:392-97; September 1961.

56. SISTER ELISE MARIE. "Developing a Writing Unit." *Catholic Educational Review* 59:83-90; February 1961.

57. SISTER MARY L. MOE. "Teaching Composition in the Seventh Grade." *Dissertation Abstracts* 16:920; No. 5; 1956. 16 p.

58. SPARKS, J. E. "Real-Life Writing Assignments." *NEA Journal* 44:27; January 1955.

59. STENSLAND, ANNA LEE. "Current Issues in the Teaching of Poetry in Secondary School." *Dissertation Abstracts* 19:1683; No. 7; 1959. 341 p.

60. STRICKLAND, RUTH G. "Evaluating Children's Composition." *Elementary English* 37:321-30; May 1960.

61. STRICKLAND, RUTH G. *Language Arts in the Elementary School.* Second edition. Boston: D. C. Heath & Co., 1957.

62. STROM, INGRID M. "Research in Teaching Grammar and Usage." *Education Digest* 26:50-52; January 1961.

63. SUGGS, LENA REDDICK. "Structural Grammar Versus Traditional Grammar in Influencing Writing." *English Journal* 50:174-78; March 1961.

64. TORRANCE, ELLIS P. *Guiding Creative Talent.* Englewood Cliffs, New Jersey: Prentice-Hall, Inc., 1962. 278 p.

65. WAGNER, GUY. "What Schools Are Doing in Creative Writing." *Education* 79:62-65; September 1958.

66. WITHERS, S. "Creativity in English, A Dissent." *Phi Delta Kappan* 42:311-14; April 1961.

67. WITTICK, MILDRED L. "Correctness and Freshness: Can Children's Writing Have Both?" *Elementary School Journal* 60:295-300; March 1960.

68. WITTY, PAUL A. "Some Values of Creative Writing." *Elementary English* 34:139-45; March 1957.

69. WITTY, PAUL A., and WILLIAM MARTIN. "An Analysis of Children's Compositions Written in Response to a Film." *Elementary English* 34:158-63; March 1957.

Chapter Five

The Old Demon: Spelling

WEBSTER first published his renowned spelling book in 1782. Originally it bore the imposing title, *The First Part of a Grammatical Institute of the English Language.* Later, in 1817, it appeared bearing the title, *American Spelling Book,* and in 1829 was issued as the *Elementary Spelling Book* —the famous "Old Blue-Back Speller" that served as a mainstay of instruction in schools of the nineteenth century.

In a thinly populated United States, five million copies of Webster's spellers had been sold by 1818. From 1840 to 1880 a million copies per year were marketed, and as late as 1946 a 5,000-copy edition was snapped up by nostalgic collectors. With so much emphasis on orthography infused in our national bloodstream for generations, it is little wonder that teachers and parents alike have remained interested in how well children spell.

Teachers' interests in research in spelling. The impression that children and youth do not spell well, an impression to which research has given some support, was frequently voiced during the past decade when instructional methods were under heavy fire. Such criticisms undoubtedly led teachers to ask questions about research in spelling that centered around (a) current trends and opinions bearing on spelling practices, (b) the matter of what makes a good speller *good,* (c) the role of phonics, and above all, (d) what does research say about improving methods of instruction in spelling.

It is around the four points suggested here that the present chapter is organized.

Opinions and General Comment with a Bearing on Spelling: Reviews of Research

During the past six or eight years, a substantial number of authors have addressed their remarks toward the general improvement of spelling. These writings tended to be subjective or were based on research which was *reviewed* rather than *done* by the commentators.

General comment. Articles that fall into the "editorial" category were typified by a *Newsweek* (22) item cryptically entitled "C-A-T," which viewed with concern the apparent decline of spelling ability displayed by college freshmen between 1943 and 1954. Data cited had been compiled from 52 colleges in 27 states by two professors from the University of Illinois and New York University.

Horn (76) reviewed issues in spelling, and Furness (51) dealt with five forces that perpetuate "illogical and inconsistent" spelling as the "5 P's": Printers, Professional writers, Public perversity and pride, Pronunciation, and Prestige. Furness (46) also looked at knotty problems of spelling in an article published earlier than the one just cited.

Johnson (83) stressed meanings and word structure patterns as key factors influencing spelling. Bush (18) spoke of the importance of motivation, while Blake (10) advocated more individualized teaching, since children learn to spell in different ways.

Other general statements with respect to improving spelling recently were made by Horn (70), who listed experiences that improve spelling; Hatfield (67), who suggested why some students spell poorly; Gates (61), who preserved objectives for improved spelling programs; and Schuyler (116), Wehr (130), and Brendel (16), who proposed ways of improving pupil performance.

Carlsen (20), Sandmeyer (115), and Boyer (14) dealt with the individual speller's problems while Jones and Holder (84) described what had been done in Richmond, Indiana, to improve spelling in both elementary and secondary levels. The last-named reference moved beyond editorial opinion per se by drawing on findings from a three-year spelling improvement venture.

Among other general articles were those by Parke (100), Feigenbaun (34), and Spache (124). Feigenbaun called for alphabet reforms, pointing out that there are 251 ways of spelling 44 sounds in our language.

Opinions based on research reviews. Betts (9) listed causes of spelling deficiencies, factors to consider in remedial programs, and sources of children's confusion. Eight causes of spelling deficiencies were given as:

1. Limited mental ability
2. Limited reading ability
3. Hearing impairment
4. Visual defects
5. Faulty listening skills
6. Poor handwriting
7. Overemphasis of phonics
8. Poor study habits.

Among Betts' dozen sources of children's confusion were spelling before reading, learning difficult words too soon, letter-by-letter spelling, isolating parts of words, and memorization of rules.

Furness (54) surveyed research to identify reasons "Why John Can't Spell" and Strickland (126) eloquently discussed the importance of utilizing spelling research. Fitzgerald (35) proposed a seven-step evaluation process for appraising ability, progress, and achievement, while Gallagher (60) commented on the supervision of the teaching of spelling. Furness (52) also concerned herself with the improvement of spelling in the high school.

Reviews of research in spelling. Some writers, in recent years, have provided an important service for individual students and school systems by compiling and interpreting research in spelling. Horn's (73) bulletin published by the NEA is an example of a helpful general treatise, as is the section of the 1960 *Encyclopedia of Educational Research* entitled "Spelling," which Horn (72) also contributed. Among his concluding comments was this: ". . . the chief problem today appears to be a more critical and universal application of the evidence now available" (72:1350).

DeBoer (31) completed an excellent review of research in 1961, and Wittick (134) provided lists of spelling references in recent issues of *Elementary School Journal*. A compilation of research, including work in spelling, brought together selected and significant research of recent decades in a 1958 volume edited by Hunnicutt and Iverson (78), *Research in the Three R's*. Enduring and sometimes hard-to-get materials are included.

A doctoral thesis by Pavlak (101) analyzed and evaluated research in general spelling methods. He compiled a 234-item bibliography that covered a 30-year period. Both bibliography and findings are of interest.

One of Horn's (75) more recent articles on research in spelling serves to round out this section. Six points that he gleaned from his review are as follows:

1. The spelling program should be structured around a central writing core of from two to three thousand words.

2. From the intermediate grades and upward throughout school, composition, creative writing, and dictionary study skills should be provided and so arranged as to carry a major part of the instructional load.

3. The list presentation of words is more efficient than contextual presentation.

4. The test-study method is superior to the study-test method of instruction.

5. The corrected test technique (part of test-study approach) is the most efficient single procedure for learning to spell.

6. Marking the hard spots in words has little or no value. The most promising form of word analysis appears to relate to suffixes.

What Makes a Good Speller Good?

The spectrum of human differences. Since it long has been self-evident that the spelling ability of children in a given age range varies conspicuously, it is quite natural that teachers should be concerned with research that may offer clues as to why children differ in the power to spell. At least a modest handful of studies throw light on the question of why some children learn to spell more rapidly than others in a similar school situation.

Richmond (108), working with sixth grade children, prepared a readable interpretation of their spelling needs. Among the data—a core of approximately 2,500 words comprised 95 percent of the vocabulary children used in writing.

Russell (112) again has reported on the characteristics of good and poor spellers. He concluded that poor spelling ability in grades five and six is closely related to poor auditory discrimination and visual differences, although high spelling ability is not necessarily related to superior discrimination. Furness (45) emphasized the importance of correct pronunication—including articulation, enunciation, and syllabification. She also has commented elsewhere (47) on psychological determinants of spelling success as suggested by research. Among her points were these:

1. Ability to spell seems to be contingent upon two processes—recognition and reproduction.

2. Imagery appears to be involved in spelling but teachers and psychologists are still uncertain of its role.

3. Relationship between intelligence and spelling ability is much lower than that found between intelligence and most other school subjects.

4. There is an emotional factor involved in spelling difficulty. The older the child, the more difficulties and discouragements encountered, but these old attitudes can be replaced with new ones.

5. Indifference, carelessness, and distaste for intellectual drudgery are major factors in poor spelling, especially with the student with a high I. Q.

6. To be a good speller, an individual must first develop a "spelling conscience."

7. "The skillful management of incentives is unquestionably more important than techniques of instruction."

An experiment involving control and experimental groups with 33 children in each was conducted by Carrell and Pendergast (21). Their purpose was to ascertain whether there was a relationship between errors in speech and in spelling. Although 37,625 words were analyzed for spelling errors during the study, no particular evidence was found to support the common assumption that speech errors and spelling errors are directly or indirectly related.

71

On the other hand, Russell (111) found that auditory abilities and spelling achievement, at the primary level, did appear to be related. He reported that:

1. Some auditory abilities are significantly related to spelling abilities at the 1 percent level of confidence.

2. Some verbal auditory skills are significantly related to both spelling and reading ability; these abilities involved recognition of word parts rather than whole words.

3. Relationship of listening comprehension of paragraphs to spelling scores was much lower.

4. Considerable contribution to spelling variance was unaccounted for, indicating the possibility that visual discrimination factors may be important in spelling or that a wider range of specific kinds of auditory skills should be tested probably in relation to both spelling and reading.

In the same general vein, Damgaard (29) worked on auditory acuity and discrimination differences in spelling. Her conclusions included the point that the pitch, loudness, and rhythm with which spelling words were presented influenced results. Timbre of the teacher's voice and the sex of the pupil did not influence results.

Rea (107) studied oral-aural training with 207 second graders as subjects. Among her other findings in the study, she made the point that the teaching of principles in regard to the application of phonemes in contextual writing did produce greater transfer of learning to similar tasks than was evidenced by training which emphasized either the visual or the haptical [1] approach.

Weislogel's (131) doctoral study, done at the adult level, viewed the relationship between visual memory and spelling. She wrote that ". . . the hypothesis of a high relationship between spelling and visual memory is defined in terms of the tests used in this study." (The Lincoln Diagnostic Spelling Test and the Cooperative English Test were used.)

Among highly specialized studies germane to spelling were two done by Thurston (128) and by Holmes and Hyman (69). The former dealt with the loss of spelling ability in dysphasics [2] who performed far below normal subjects. Holmes and Hyman, in a veterans' hospital, made a case study of spelling disability and asyntaxia [3] in a case involving injury to the language formation area of the brain.

---

[1] The term "haptical" means relating to or based on the sense of touch.

[2] The dysphasic is one with an impaired ability to speak, or sometimes, to understand language due to brain injury.

[3] "Asyntactical" means "not syntactical." *Asyntaxia* refers to the condition of a person incapable of successfully utilizing conventional word order, hence given to garbled speech, due to linguistic loss occasioned by damage to the language formation area of the brain.

To sum up, considerable piecemeal evidence has accumulated with respect to probable causes of spelling difficulty, and inferentially, as to the reasons why certain persons learn to spell more readily than others. Psychological and physiological factors involved are gradually being clarified, but we are far short of reaching broad, definitive conclusions.

Spelling in relation to reading. Just as certain research workers viewed reading in the context of other fields (cf. Chapter Two), so certain students have interested themselves in spelling-reading relationships. Since studies reviewed in the 1955 ASCD booklet, *Research Helps in Teaching the Language Arts* (118:53), already support this relationship, little more needs be adduced here.

Furness (49), for instance, reported that there is a correlation between reading and spelling test scores of .80 and .85, as compared to a .30 to .40 relationship between intelligence and spelling. Also, there are many skills and abilities common to both subjects, such as (a) the same basis for vocabulary; (b) ability to recognize and remember words; (c) word study; (d) accuracy and speed of visual perception; (e) auditory discrimination; and (f) phonic skills. In reading, one proceeds from the written word through the spoken form to the meaning, while in spelling, however, the procedure is from meaning to the written symbol.

Intelligence, Furness concludes, is important for achievement in spelling and reading; but vocabulary, perception, word recognition, word analysis, comprehension, and phonics are more important.

In grades three through eight, an effort was made by Morrison and Perry (94) to measure the relationship between spelling and general reading ability in 840 children. The outcome was of interest (94:226):

. . . the tendency for more retardation to be found in spelling than in reading in the third and fourth grades suggests a need for more emphasis on readiness for spelling. The degree of readiness of the pupils, the kinds of teaching procedures, and the quality of the teaching seem to have an important effect on the quality of the learning which results. From the large degree of retardation in both spelling and reading and the tendency for this retardation to persist and increase, the question arises as to whether or not the lack of basic skills in comprehension and interpretation in reading and basic skills in spelling tend to interfere with the acquisition of newer skills and that the entire problem may be intensified by the frustration and discouragement of the learner.

Points made by Stauffer (125), slightly paraphrased, anent spelling and reading were that:

1. Reading and spelling are two facets of the language arts, not discrete fields.

2. The correlations between reading and spelling are relatively high.

3. The best single measure of a child's readiness for reading is how well he talks.

4. Spelling rules, like phonetics, should never be taught in isolation.

5. Self-study skills are important in spelling and reading.

6. For best results, spelling instruction should be coordinated with instruction in the different curriculum areas.

7. As a rule of thumb, avoid asking a child to spell a word he cannot read, regardless of the curriculum area in which it occurs.

Particularly prolific in writing with respect to spelling in recent years, Furness (43) makes several points that are applicable to both spelling and reading. She holds that spelling readiness is a mental and physical state of development or maturation which makes it possible for a learner to spell at his appropriate level without excessive strain or difficulty. It is difficult to determine, she notes, whether single causation or a combination of factors is the more responsible for the spelling readiness of the individual child.

Phonics and Word Recognition

The role of phonic skill development in spelling instruction remains somewhat in the controversial realm, but the *incidence* of research reports which recognize or stress the importance of phonics has increased recently.

General viewpoints. Foley (39) examined various arguments for and against the phonetically simplified spelling of English words but made no drastic suggestions for phonetic reformation. Fitzgerald (36) sustained the importance of phonics in spelling, and Pecozzi (103) described a program of phonic instruction in an article with the cheerful title, "Spelling Can Be Fun." For his part, Horn (71) listed six types of evidence which he believed should be appraised in considering the potential contributions of phonic instruction to spelling. His usual judicious advice includes the comment that children should learn the ways in which each sound is spelled. Also, they should learn how to spell the principal prefixes and suffixes and how to add these to base words. They should learn such orthographic aids as apply to large numbers of words. Finally, says Horn, help may be gotten from knowledge of word patterns, but there is no avoiding direct teaching of the large number of common words which do not conform in their spelling to any orthographic or phonetic rule.

Indefatigably scanning and interpreting research, Furness (42) has done a useful job of compiling, in *Clearing House* magazine, a list of points which pertain to phonics instruction and spelling success. Listing about a dozen items, her succinct presentation of research data is most useful.

Cf. footnote on p. 14 for definitions of *phonics* and *phonetics*.

Pro and con. Probably no one denies that there is a place for phonic instruction. Yet the nature, timing, and extent of phonics in spelling add up to a compound issue.

Cook (28) compared the each-word-as-a-whole approach with the early phonetic-structural analysis (workbook) approach. Thirty-eight class-rooms enrolled the 983 Minnesota children who participated, 437 of the youngsters being in her control (basic word list) group. Neither of Cook's methods produced proportionately more poor spellers than did the other, but mean scores made on the final spelling tests showed a statistically significant difference in favor of the control (word list) group.

A substantial number of research-based articles directly or indirectly supported some stress on phonic instruction at certain grade levels. Among those reporting were Aaron (1), Willging (133), Holmes (68), Templin (127), and Newton (97). Statements abstracted from their writings include the following:

Ability in the spelling of phonetic syllables seems to be predictive of spelling achievement. (Aaron)

Children were attracted to and could cope with passages of English rewritten more phonetically. (Willging)

Spelling ability at the high school and university level depends to a large extent upon ability to handle phonetic association. (Holmes)

Correlations between phonic knowledge and spelling are somewhat higher than between phonic knowledge and reading. (Templin)

Of the abilities and skills investigated in this problem, the ability to spell phonetic syllables is the greatest contributor. (Newton)

Although quoted out of context, the preceding excerpts *do* reflect faithfully the present temperate and somewhat favorable climate with respect to phonics. Numerous other points were made by the researchers cited.

Petty (104) attacked the problem of whether or not there was a relationship between the persistence of spelling difficulties in socially useful words and the presence of certain phonetic elements in these words. Among his summarizing statements were these: (a) for the words tested there appeared to be no recognizable patterns for misspelling as evidenced by the wide range of misspellings for each word; and (b) the phonemes selected for study which seemed to indicate a relationship to the persistence of spelling difficulty of the words containing them do not show directly such relationship. Petty inferred from his study that emphasis should be placed on learning each word as an individual problem.

Syllabication [5] and word recognition. Closely allied to phonics inquiries were studies in syllabication and word recognition. Chase (24) learned

[5] Also spelled *syllabification.*

that the word recognition abilities she tested in spelling overachievers were significantly different from those of underachievers, while Mason (92) tackled the problem of whether word discrimination could be taught as an isolated process, and if so, whether spelling skill consequently could be increased. Using 107 Victoria, British Columbia, youngsters in four sixth grades as experimental groups, he found that their progress exceeded (at the .01 level of confidence) the performance of 97 children in four control groups. Presumably, therefore, word discrimination was taught with concomitant enhancement of spelling skill.

Horn (74) has made reference to the fact that evidence is inconclusive as to any negative effects of the syllabic presentation of words and suggested that attention to syllabic elements was desirable but *not* as a regular or basic method of learning to spell. Osburn (98), in seeming disagreement, proposed that, in teaching spelling, a main problem is to help pupils learn how to spell the syllables they will most often need. He identified 50 "key syllables" of importance for this purpose and expressed the view that syllabication skill is more vital in spelling than in reading.

Otterman (99), after working with 585 seventh graders in a two-group study, concluded that 30 ten-minute lessons on prefixes and root words improved spelling scores appreciably for the experimental (prefix-root word) group.

Bloomer (13) examined word length and complexity as factors in spelling difficulty and verified a number of common impressions of teachers, namely that:

1. The longer a word is the more difficult it is.
2. Words with double vowels are especially hard.
3. Words with double consonants seem difficult to spell.
4. Words with hyphens and apostrophes are more difficult to spell.
5. The teacher should pronounce the vowels in a word carefully and be sure that the child knows the different sounds of each.

Few persons are likely to disagree vehemently with Bloomer's position!

Presumably children methodically can be helped to develop spelling ability outside the frame of conventional spelling instruction. These agreeable conclusions were suggested by Baker's (5) work with young adolescents (15 to 18 years old) in history classes.

As a concluding generalization, it seems quite safe to say that *deliberate* instruction in spelling (as distinct from a casual, incidental, or "experience-centered" approach) pays off in the form of improved test scores. By the same token, the success of methodical teaching should not be construed so as to minimize the value of enrichment experiences, individual word lists, or other devices and procedures that can keep spelling from becoming a rote learning or drill-centered task that deadens several hours in the classroom each week. Ways of vitalizing spelling are suggested in the next section.

The Improvement of Spelling Instruction Through Better Teaching Methods

The largest single cluster of publications pertaining to spelling dealt with ways of improving instruction. These writings proved to be loosely divided among various subdivisions. These were general research statements containing sage advice, research reports (a number from the field of business education), a few writings concerned with teaching aids, suggested methods based on spelling games, attempts to identify spelling demons, and proposals for improving remedial instruction.

"Sage advice." A number of commentators expressed *opinions* as to how spelling can most rapidly be improved. Among those with general advice to offer were Burrows (17), Sister Mary Catherine (122), Pounds (106), and Marshall (89). Each contributed analytical and common-sense points.

In a similar vein were three articles by Furness (50; 44; 48), who wrote about "dos and don'ts" of spelling, about diagnosis, and about spelling in the high school. Barbe (6) listed important considerations in spelling, and Bremer (15) listed several ways of improving instruction. Morris (93) suggested helpful rules, as did Wagner (129), while Chappel (23) dealt with explicit procedures in the classroom at the primary level. All of the dozen reports cited should prove useful to teachers who are concerned with alleviating the "daily spelling grind" with an infusion of fresh ideas.

The importance of motivation, in broad terms, was reiterated by Christ (25) and by Petty and Plessas (105). The last two named were concerned with the need to stimulate children who already spelled well and who might be in danger of losing interest in routine tasks.

Research and methodology. The student interested in changes transpiring in our language will enjoy Horn's (77) efforts to identify new words seeping into common use. Taking letters written to editors of popular magazines and newspapers as sources of data, Horn found a trend toward the use of initials—FBI and GI, for instance—and toward compound words (carpool; babysitter). Out of the 22,485 words checked in the late 1950s, however, all but 216 were listed by Webster as far back as 1923. The minting of new words occurs slowly, or so it seems, but the development of new meanings and extended meanings is increasing.

An equally beguiling study was Wilkinson's (132) inventory of student teachers' spelling errors. With the exception of one word, errors of future teachers coincided with children's mistakes.

Blitz (11) described an individualized spelling program, developed at the fifth grade level, in explicit detail. On the other side of the coin, Deacon (30), using matched groups, studied standardized versus personal word lists in spelling and warned that spelling can become too individualized! His standard-list group excelled in achievement gains, and he was led to recommend a standardized list *plus* a "build your own list" approach.

Other comparative studies of interest were made by Beatty (8), Hahn (66), Calhoun (19), and Delacato (32). The test-study-test approach was compared with the study-test method by Beatty who learned that the "better" approach varied with the experimental settings. Hahn's work was done with 848 pupils in grades three to six in comparing contextual versus column spelling. Among his findings:

1. The contextual method is at least as effective as the column method in teaching pupils to spell words correctly, either in column or context.

2. The elimination of phonics drill in the contextual method does not result in lower spelling achievement by pupils.

3. The contextual method contains no inherent difficulty for pupils because of their sex, ability, or socio-economic background.

4. The contextual method is as efficient as the column method in reference to time required for teaching and the amount of work required of teachers.

5. The attitude of pupils when taught by the contextual method is more favorable than when taught by the column method.

"Intensive" spelling was compared with "conventional" methods by Calhoun, the results being favorable to the former procedure. Delacato's formal-versus-informal-methods study, a five-year inquiry, led him to note that the informal, typical, and intensive approaches to the teaching of spelling all have strengths and weaknesses, none of them being ideal or a total approach.

"Action" and "cooperative" projects for improving spelling were described by Ahrens (2) and Rilling (109). Sandberg (113) reported that repetitive writing of words misspelled—an old method, indeed—assisted college students in Iowa to reduce errors by 50 percent, and Foster (40), working with high school pupils, described a plan for motivating spelling through three five-minute periods each week. In short, during recent seasons just about every approach imaginable has been employed in one school situation or another! One further case in point: Goss (64) taught proofreading to experimental groups in an Oklahoma study that enrolled a total of 543 children. After 12 weeks the spelling of the young proofreaders improved significantly, while that of pupils in control groups did not.

Space permits mention of only a few more examples of research-based reports that dwelt on methods or procedures. Murphy and LeBaron (95) selected core words for the New York State spelling list by surveying errors made by eighth graders. Kyte (86) analyzed intermediate grade spelling errors and noted that faulty handwriting accounted for many mistakes. Laycock (88) found, in a sample of 100 college freshmen, a negligible relationship between their individual spelling abilities and their vocabularies. Also, Coard (26), testing freshmen, found that the students themselves most often blamed carelessness, haste, and laziness for their errors. By their own testimony, students identified indifference as the greatest obstacle to better levels of performance.

Business schools report . . . In recent years the field of business education has become the source of data related to spelling. Two studies, both by Jensen and Jensen (81; 82), adduce some evidence that shorthand study does not have an adverse effect on spelling scores. Sanders (114) described a four-year National Office Management Association project for improving spelling, and Larson (87) enumerated techniques that apparently proved successful in a West Coast secretarial school. Analogous efforts to strengthen spelling in business education were described by DiLoreto and Perkins (33) and by Royer (110).

Reports of the sort previously mentioned have tended to be descriptive rather than experimental but generally were based on performance records kept when new programs were initiated.

Tapes and tachistoscopes. Major reports dealing with "teaching machines" of the newer type had yet to filter into the literature concerned with spelling by 1961-62. Experiments with tape recorders and tachistoscopes, however, were described.

Work with the tachistoscope in spelling instruction was described and reviewed by Beacon (7), who felt that her fifth grade children profited from the word-recognition experiences involved. Progress records were kept methodically throughout a two-year interval.

The use of tapes at the seventh grade level proved to be effective at the close of a study by Peckrel et al. (102). Subsequent follow-up experimentation by Gibson (63) in the same junior-senior high school in Nebraska confirmed the point that tape-taught pupils spelled better than those who were teacher-supervised. Later, Gibson (62) recounted the extension of tape-teaching to include instruction in conversational Spanish. The performance of secondary school children in foreign language classes was not as markedly improved through the use of tapes as was spelling performance.

Spelling games. The spelling bee continues to buzz along as an instructional device. In fact, judging by articles in print, the spelling-game enthusiasts are, if anything, more numerous than ever.

Sister Mary Loyola (123), Jencka (80), and Kelly (85) are among those who described spell-downs and spelling bees with new twists and ideas. Coard (27) supported spelling games at the secondary level, and Anderson (3) described five "spelling games that teach" in one journal and ten intermediate grade games in another (4).

Spelling demons and word lists. The identification of spelling "demons" —troublesome words like *desiccate* or *consensus*—remains a popular pastime. Furness and Boyd in particular seem to have had a field-day in tagging demons. Among their writings in the past three or four years:

1. The compilation of a 98-word list for high school study (56; 57)
2. A listing of "231 Real Spelling Demons" for secondary students (59)
3. A list of "335 Real Spelling Demons" for university age students (58)
4. Eighteen demon-lists containing 1,302 different words that contain "hard spots" for high school students (55).

Scott and Wilson (117) have evaluated a particular speller in relationship to four standard spelling tests and word-list research, and Fitzgerald (37; 38) dealt with the selection of words appropriate for spelling lists.

A New Zealand Council for Educational Research bulletin (96) may be of some interest to United States readers. An appraisal is made therein of a new program in spelling which, at the time the bulletin was issued, had been in effect for four years. The system being tried out apparently is based on the premise that children are more likely to learn to spell words they use while writing on topics of interest—even if the words are more difficult than those on official lists.

Remedial work in spelling. Individual remedial help in spelling has been described by Sheppard (120), and effective remedial methods were discussed by Jans (79).

A business education study by Martin (90) reviewed causes of poor spelling in high schools and colleges, proposed remedial techniques, and detailed steps taken under his direction to help students in a Michigan town. Finally, a readable article by Furness (53) identified certain spelling difficulties encountered by younger children and proposed possible ways of approaching and overcoming these.

Summary

Although many publications have dealt with spelling during the past five or six years, the research data preserved in such articles leave unanswered a large number of the how-do-I-do-it questions raised by teachers. Many reports are limited, some are conflicting, while others add bricks to the frame of knowledge but leave the structure far from complete.

Albert Camus once said that "Great ideas come into the world as gently as doves. Perhaps if we listen attentively we shall hear, amid the uproar of empires and nations, a faint flutter of wings, the gentle stirring of life and hope." Among the writings that deal with spelling, there unquestionably are good ideas temperately voiced. If the teacher listens attentively, these should help him to do a better job. Especially important is the *personal* task of the teacher: to piece together from many comments and viewpoints —from gentle stirrings of ideas and from research—the kinds of experiences in spelling that improve learning.

Bibliography

1. AARON, IRA EDWARD. "The Relationship of Selected Measures at the Fourth and Eighth Grade Levels." *Journal of Educational Research* 53:138-43; December 1959.
2. AHRENS, MAURICE R. "Improved Spelling Through Action Research." *Instructor* 67:6; May 1958.
3. ANDERSON, PAUL S. "Spelling Games That Teach." *NEA Journal* 46:398; September 1957.
4. ANDERSON, PAUL S. "Ten Spelling Games for the Intermediate Grades." *Grade Teacher* 73:57; May 1956.
5. BAKER, JANET. "Mastery of Vocabulary in History." *Journal of Educational Research* 50:589-95; April 1957.
6. BARBE, WALTER B. "Spelling To Learn." *Education* 76:303-305; January 1956.
7. BEACON, FRANCES MANN. "We Improved Spelling with the Tachistoscope." *Educational Screen* 35:408; November 1956.
8. BEATTY, DOROTHY M. "A Comparison of Two Methods of Teaching Spelling." Unpublished doctoral thesis. Iowa City: State University of Iowa, 1955. 320 p. Typed.
9. BETTS, EMMETT A. "What About Spelling?" *Education* 76:310-25; January 1956.
10. BLAKE, HOWARD E. "Studying Spelling Independently." *Elementary English* 37:29-32; January 1960.
11. BLITZ, THEODORE F. "Experiment in Individualized Spelling." *Elementary English* 31:403-407; November 1954.
12. BLOOMER, RICHARD H. "Concepts of Meaning and the Reading and Spelling Difficulty of Words." *Journal of Educational Research* 54:178-82; January 1961.
13. BLOOMER, RICHARD H. "Word Length and Complexity Variables in Spelling Difficulty." *Journal of Educational Research* 49:531-35; March 1956.
14. BOYER, HARVEY KINSEY. "Why You Can't Spell." *Science Digest* 37:83-86; January 1955.
15. BREMER, NEVILLE H. "Ways To Improve Spelling in the Elementary Grades." *Elementary English* 38:301-307; May 1961.
16. BRENDEL, LEROY ANDREW. "Integrate Your Spelling, Punctuation, and Proofreading Program." *Business Education World* 37:15-17; February 1957. 37:33-35; March 1957.
17. BURROWS, ALVINA T. "Spelling and Composition." *Education* 79:211-18; December 1958.

18. BUSH, JARVIS E. "Motivation for Learning To Spell." *English Journal* 43:34-35; January 1954.

19. CALHOUN, ROBERT T. "Comparison of a Typical and an Intensive Method of Teaching Spelling." *Elementary School Journal* 55:154-57; November 1954.

20. CARLSEN, GEORGE ROBERT. "So They Still Can't Spell." *Education* 79:219-24; December 1958.

21. CARRELL, JAMES AUBREY, and K. K. PENDERGAST. "Experimental Study of the Possible Relation Between Errors of Speech and Spelling." *Journal of Speech and Hearing Disorders* 19:327-34; September 1954.

22. "C-A-T." *Newsweek* 43:66; June 14, 1954.

23. CHAPPEL, BERNICE M. "Do Your Second Graders Say, 'I Don't Like Spelling'?" *Instructor* 66:68, 72; September 1956.

24. CHASE, NAOMI C. "A Comparative Study of the Word Recognition Abilities of Good and Poor Spellers in the Third Grade." Unpublished doctoral thesis. Minneapolis: University of Minnesota, 1958. 247 p. Typed.

25. CHRIST, FRANK L. "Motivating Your Students To Spell Better." *Clearing House* 35:173; November 1960.

26. COARD, ROBERT L. "Mystery of Misspelling." *Elementary School Journal* 58:97-100; November 1957.

27. COARD, ROBERT L. "Spelling Game Time." *Clearing House* 30:9-10; September 1955.

28. COOK, RUTH C. "Evaluation of Two Methods of Teaching Spelling." *Elementary School Journal* 58:21-27; October 1957.

29. DAMGAARD, THELMA L. J. "Auditory Acuity and Discrimination Differences as Factors in Spelling Competence." Unpublished doctoral thesis. Stanford, California: Stanford University, 1956. 69 p.

30. DEACON, LAWRENCE S. "Teaching of Spelling Can Become Too Individualized." *Education* 76:300-302; January 1956.

31. DEBOER, JOHN JAMES. "Composition, Handwriting, and Spelling: The Teaching of Spelling." *Review of Educational Research* 31:167-68; April 1961.

32. DELACATO, CARL H. "Spelling: Five-Year Study." *Elementary English* 32:296-98; May 1955.

33. DILORETO, A., and E. A. PERKINS. "These Two Methods May Solve Students' Spelling Problems." *Business Education World* 41:22-23; May 1961.

34. FEIGENBAUN, LAWRENCE H. "For a Bigger and Better Alphabet." *High Points* 40:34-36; May 1958.

35. FITZGERALD, JAMES AUGUSTINE. "Evaluation of Spelling Ability, Progress and Achievement." *Education* 77:404-408; March 1957.

36. FITZGERALD, JAMES AUGUSTINE. "Problems and Issues in Spelling." *National Catholic Educational Association Bulletin* 53:7-30; February 1957.

37. FITZGERALD, JAMES AUGUSTINE. "Selection of Vocabulary for Basic Spelling Instruction." *Education* 76:286-90; January 1956.

38. FITZGERALD, JAMES AUGUSTINE. "What Words Should Children Study in Spelling?" *Education* 79:224-28; December 1958.

39. FOLEY, LOUIS. "Doctor of Letters." *Phi Delta Kappan* 42:316-21; April 1961.

40. FOSTER, GUY L. "Fifteen Minutes a Week for Motivated Spelling." *Clearing House* 29:48-49; September 1954.

41. FREDENBURGH, FRANZ A. "Does Togetherness Work in the Classroom?" *Elementary School Journal* 62:42-45; October 1961.

42. FURNESS, EDNA L. "Evidence on Phonics Instruction and Spelling Success." *Clearing House* 31:279-83; January 1957.

43. FURNESS, EDNA L. "Factors in Spelling Readiness." *Educational Administration and Supervision* 41:440-45; November 1955.

44. FURNESS, EDNA L. "It's Time To Diagnose Spelling Troubles." *Clearing House* 32:390-92; March 1958.

45. FURNESS, EDNA L. "Mispronunciations, Mistakes, and Methods in Spelling." *Elementary English* 33:508-11; December 1956.

46. FURNESS, EDNA L. "Pink Pills for a Pale Spelling Situation." *American School Board Journal* 133:17-18; July 1956.

47. FURNESS, EDNA L. "Psychological Determinants of Spelling Success." *Education* 79:234-39; December 1958.

48. FURNESS, EDNA L. "Retooling the High School Spelling Program." *American School Board Journal* 133:29-30; September 1956.

49. FURNESS, EDNA L. "Should Reading and Spelling Be Taught Separately?" *Clearing House* 31:67-70; October 1956.

50. FURNESS, EDNA L. "Some Do's and Do Not's for Spelling." *Elementary English* 31:407-409; November 1954.

51. FURNESS, EDNA L. "Spelling: Illogical and Inconsistent." *Clearing House* 33:330-33; February 1959.

52. FURNESS, EDNA L. "Sputniks, Science, and Spelling." *American School Board Journal* 136:36-37; March 1958.

53. FURNESS, EDNA L. "Teaching Procedures for Spelling Disabilities." *Elementary English* 31:158-62+; March 1954.

54. FURNESS, EDNA L. "Why John Can't Spell." *School and Society* 82:199-202; December 24, 1955.

55. FURNESS, EDNA L., and G. A. BOYD. *Hard Spots in Hard Words for Secondary School Students.* College of Education Bulletin, No. 4. Laramie: University of Wyoming, April 1958. 27 p.

56. FURNESS, EDNA L., and G. A. BOYD. "Learn To Spell First Words First." *Educational Administration and Supervision* 45:49-53; January 1959.

57. FURNESS, EDNA L., and G. A. BOYD. "Ninety-Eight Spelling Demons for High School and College Students." *Educational Administration and Supervision* 44:353-56; November 1958.

58. FURNESS, EDNA L., and G. A. BOYD. "335 Real Spelling Demons for College Students." *College English* 20:292-95; March 1959.

59. FURNESS, EDNA L., and G. A. BOYD. "231 Real Spelling Demons for High School Students." *English Journal* 47:267-70; May 1958.

60. GALLAGHER, SISTER MARIE THERESA. "Supervision of the Teaching of Spelling." *National Catholic Educational Association Bulletin* 53:31-39; February 1957.

61. GATES, ARTHUR I. "Developing the Basic Spelling Techniques in the Language Arts Program." *Education* 76:275-79; January 1956.

62. GIBSON, ROMAIN. "Can Tapes Teach?" *Education Screen* 37:180-81; April 1957.

63. GIBSON, ROMAIN. "Tape Recordings Experiment Is Expanded in Westside Junior and Senior High Schools." *National Association of Secondary-School Principals Bulletin* 43:49-72; January 1959.

64. GOSS, JAMES E. "Analysis of Accuracy of Spelling in Written Compositions of Elementary School Children and the Effects of Proofreading Emphasis upon Accuracy." Unpublished doctoral thesis. Norman: University of Oklahoma, 1959. 107 p. Typed.

65. GROFF, PATRICK J. "The New Iowa Spelling Scale: How Phonic Is It?" *Elementary School Journal* 62:46-49; October 1961.

66. HAHN, WILLIAM PAUL. "Comparative Efficiency of the Teaching of Spelling by the Column and Contextual Methods." Unpublished doctoral thesis. Pittsburgh: University of Pittsburgh, 1960. 145 p. Typed.

67. HATFIELD, WALTER WILBER. "Why Some Pupils Can't Spell and What To Do About It." *Instructor* 68:50+; November 1958.

68. HOLMES, JACK ALROY. "Substrata Analysis of Spelling Ability for Elements of Auditory Images." *Journal of Experimental Education* 22:329-41; January 1954.

69. HOLMES, JACK ALROY, and WILLIAM HYMAN. "Spelling Disability and Asyntaxia in a Case Involving Injury to the Language Formation Area of the Brain." *Journal of Educational Psychology* 48:542-50; December 1957.

70. HORN, ERNEST W. "Experiences Which Develop Spelling Ability." *NEA Journal* 43:210-11; April 1954.

71. HORN, ERNEST W. "Phonetics and Spelling." *Elementary School Journal* 57:424-32; May 1957.

72. HORN, ERNEST W. "Spelling." *Encyclopedia of Educational Research.* Chester W. Harris, editor. Third edition. New York: The Macmillan Co., 1960. p. 1337-54.

73. HORN, ERNEST W. *Teaching Spelling.* (What Research Says to the Teacher.) Department of Classroom Teachers, No. 3. Washington, D.C.: American Educational Research Association, 1954. 32 p.

74. HORN, THOMAS D. "How Syllables Can Help in Spelling." *Education* 76:291-95; January 1956.

75. HORN, THOMAS D. "Research in Spelling." *Elementary English* 37:174-77; March 1960.

76. HORN, THOMAS D. "Some Issues in Learning To Spell." *Education* 79:229-33; December 1958.

77. HORN, THOMAS D. "What's New in Words These Days?" *Education* 79:203-206; December 1958.

78. HUNNICUTT, C. W., and W. J. IVERSON, editors. *Research in the Three R's.* New York: Harper and Brothers, 1958. 446 p.

79. JANS, CECILIA. "Effective Methods in Remedial Spelling." *Instructor* 65:121; September 1955.

80. JENCKA, C. "Individual Difference in the Spell Down." *Clearing House* 30:283; January 1956.

81. JENSEN, BARRY T., and JUNNE W. JENSEN. "Shorthand Study and Spelling Abilities." *Journal of Educational Psychology* 46: 112-16; February 1955.

82. JENSEN, JUNNE W., and BARRY T. JENSEN. "Do Shorthand Students Become Poor Spellers?" *Business Education World* 38:27, 33-34; February 1958.

83. JOHNSON, ELEANOR M. "Two Key Factors in Spelling Success." *Education* 76:271-74; January 1956.

84. JONES, DAISY MARVEL, and GLENN HOLDER. "Richmond Removes Its Spelling Deficiences." *American School Board Journal* 141:27; December 1960.

85. KELLY, PHILLIP L. "Spelling Bee Modern Style." *Grade Teacher* 73:105; March 1956.

86. KYTE, GEORGE CLEVELAND. "Errors in Commonly Misspelled Words in the Intermediate Grades." *Phi Delta Kappan* 39:367-72; May 1958.

87. LARSON, GRETA LaFOLLETTE. "Our Graduates Know How To Spell." *Business Education World* 38:34-35+; October 1957.

88. LAYCOCK, FRANK. "Spelling Ability and Vocabulary Level of One Hundred College Freshmen." *Journal of Educational Psychology* 45:485-91; December 1954.

89. MARSHALL, GERTRUDE W. "On Our Own in Spelling." *Elementary English* 34:543-44; December 1957.

90. MARTIN, GEORGE E. "Remedial Instruction in Spelling." *Journal of Business Education* 31:174-76; January 1956.

91. MASON, GEOFFREY P. "Word Discrimination and Spelling." *Journal of Educational Research* 50:617-21; April 1957.

92. MASON, GEOFFREY P. "Word Discrimination Skills." *Journal of Educational Research* 55:39-40; September 1961.

93. MORRIS, J. ALLEN. "Some Spelling Rules." *Industrial Arts and Vocational Education* 43:68-69; February 1954.

94. MORRISON, IDA E., and IDA F. PERRY. "Spelling and Reading Relationships with Incidence of Retardation and Acceleration." *Journal of Educational Research* 52:222-27; February 1959.

95. MURPHY, H. GEORGE, and W. A. LEBARON. "Let's Spell It Out." *Education Digest* 20:11-13; March 1955.

96. "New Spelling System in New Zealand Public Schools." *International Bureau of Education Bulletin* 34:4th quarter, 191; 1960.

97. NEWTON, BERTHA M. "A Study of Certain Factors Related to Achievement in Spelling." *Dissertations in Education.* Columbia: University of Missouri Bulletin, Study 41, 1960. p. 134-36.

98. OSBURN, WORTH JAMES. "Teaching Spelling by Teaching Syllables and Root Words." *Elementary School Journal* 55:32-41; September 1954.

99. OTTERMAN, LOIS M. "The Value of Teaching Prefixes and Post Words." *Journal of Educational Research* 48:611-16; April 1955.

100. PARKE, MARGARET B. "New Look at Spelling." *Elementary English* 32:101-109; February 1955.

101. PAVLAK, STEPHEN E. "A Critical Analysis of Scientific Research in Spelling." Unpublished doctoral thesis. Pittsburgh: University of Pittsburgh, 1956. 246 p. Typed.

102. PECKREL, G., and OTHERS. "Tape Recordings Are Used To Teach Seventh Grade Students in Westside Junior-Senior High School." *National Association of Secondary-School Principals Bulletin* 42:81-93; January 1958.

103. PECOZZI, ADELAIDE. "Spelling Can Be Fun." *Elementary English* 36:178-79; March 1959.

104. PETTY, WALTER T. "Phonetic Elements as Factors in Spelling Difficulty." *Journal of Educational Research* 51:209-14; November 1957.

105. PETTY, WALTER T., and G. P. PLESSAS. "Challenging Superior Spellers." *Elementary School Journal* 59:154-57; December 1958.

106. POUNDS, ELENORE THOMAS. "New Ways To Teach Your Child To Spell." *Parents Magazine* 28:42, 150, 152; April 1953.

107. REA, THELMA M. "Discipline in Oral-Aural Discrimination as a Factor in Developing Power in Spelling." Unpublished doctoral thesis. Stanford, California: Stanford University, 1958. 144 p.

108. RICHMOND, ARNIE E. "Children's Spelling Needs and the Implications of Research." *Journal of Experimental Education* 29:3-21; September 1960.

109. RILLING, WILLIAM F. "Co-Operative Classroom Research in Second-Grade Spelling." *Education* 80:495-97; April 1960.

110. ROYER, B. M. "Transcription: Spelling Analysis Chart." *Business World* 34:12; May 1954.

111. RUSSELL, DAVID H. "Auditory Abilities and Achievement in Spelling in the Primary Grades." *Journal of Educational Psychology* 49:315-19; December 1958.

112. RUSSELL, DAVID H. "Second Study of the Characteristics of Good and Poor Spellers." *Journal of Educational Psychology* 46:126-41; March 1955.

113. SANDBERG, EDWIN THEODORE. "Written Repetition: Aid in Spelling Improvement." *College English* 16:305-307; February 1955.

114. SANDERS, FRANK F. "How NOMA's Spelling Project Works." *Business Education World* 39:35; September 1958.

115. SANDMEYER, KATHERINE A. "Spelling: Help or Hindrance?" *Elementary English* 35:42-44+; January 1958.

116. SCHUYLER, RUBY M. "Better Ways of Teaching Spelling: Interview." *Nation's Schools* 58:48-50; September 1956.

117. SCOTT, HELEN E., and GUY M. WILSON. "Critical Examination of Spelling Words in One Speller in Relation to Four Standardized Tests in Spelling." *Journal of Educational Research* 49:331-43; January 1956.

118. SHANE, HAROLD G. *Research Helps in Teaching the Language Arts.* Washington 6, D.C.: Association for Supervision and Curriculum Development, NEA, 1201 Sixteenth Street, N. W., 1955. 80 p.

119. SHARPE, MAIDA WOOD. "Comparison of Three Approaches to Teaching Spelling." *Elementary English* 37:317-20; May 1960.

120. SHEPPARD, LILA. "Individualized Spelling Program." *Grade Teacher* 72:33+; September 1954.

121. SISTER MARIE THERESA (GALLAGHER). "Supervision of the Teaching of Spelling." *National Catholic Educational Association Bulletin* 53:31-39; February 1957.

122. SISTER MARY CATHERINE. "How Can We Teach Spelling More Efficiently?" *Catholic School Journal* 54:99-100; March 1954.

123. SISTER MARY LOYOLA. "Stand Up Spell Down." *Elementary English* 33:162-63; March 1956.

124. SPACHE, GEORGE D. "What's Wrong with Our Teaching of Spelling?" *Education* 76:296-99; January 1956.

125. STAUFFER, RUSSELL G. "Relationship Between Spelling and Reading." *Education* 79:206-10; December 1958.

126. STRICKLAND, RUTH G. "Utilizing Spelling Research." *Childhood Education* 32:69-76; October 1955.

127. TEMPLIN, M. C. "Phonic Knowledge and Its Relation to the Spelling and Reading Achievements of Fourth Grade Pupils." *Journal of Educational Research* 47:441-54; February 1954.

128. THURSTON, JOHN R. "Empirical Investigation of the Loss of Spelling Ability in Dysphasics." *Journal of Speech and Hearing Disorders* 19:344-49; September 1954.

129. WAGNER, GUY W. "Spelling Instruction." *Education* 81:381; February 1961.

130. WEHR, SAMUEL. "Pupils vs. Spelling." *National Association of Secondary-School Principals Bulletin* 42:105-107; May 1958.

131. WEISLOGEL, MARY H. "The Relationship Between Visual Memory and Spelling Ability." Unpublished doctoral thesis. Pittsburgh: University of Pittsburgh, 1954. 69 p. Typed.

132. WILKINSON, RACHEL D. "Spelling Errors of Future Teachers." *Journal of Educational Research* 51:701-705; May 1958.

133. WILLGING, HERBERT M. "On Phonetic Spelling." *Journal of Teacher Education* 7:355-59; December 1956.

134. WITTICK, MILDRED LETTON. "Selected References on Elementary School Instruction: Language Arts." *Elementary School Journal* 60:104-10; November 1959. 61:107-12; November 1960.

Chapter Six

Grammar and Usage

S KILL in communication has come to be recognized as a matter of great importance. Leaders in government and business, in the sciences, arts, and humanities are of one accord in acknowledging that the communicating of meaning must be improved in a world in which the technical means of communication have improved far more rapidly than has intelligibility.

But having agreed on the *significance* of accurate receptive and expressive communication, the advocates of improvement in the interchange of verbal and visual symbols often fail to agree as to the *means* by which this best can be done. With regard to grammar and usage, what shall our educational policies be in introducing children and youth to the system of word structures and arrangements that govern proper speaking and writing in English?

Teachers want to know . . . Prior to the preparation of this report, as frequently has been pointed out, many teachers were asked to indicate what kinds of information they deemed most valuable in improving language arts instruction in their classrooms. With respect to grammar and usage, the following were among the queries most often voiced:

1. What are national trends in practice and what are some research findings that relate to grammar and usage and that suggest how to improve instruction?

2. Are there any new developments in the controversy between the proponents of formal grammar and the advocates of the so-called "functional" approach?

3. Is teacher education now involving more preparation in English usage?

4. What are current developments with respect to semantics and linguistics with a bearing on grammar?

The pages which follow consider these points plus additional information that may be of interest to the reader.

Broad Comment

A few articles, mention of which immediately follows, are readable general commentaries on grammar and usage. Applegate (4) did her usual literate job in an article concerned with ways in which language arts teachers could make mechanics serve ideas. Representative of her "common sense" points were (a) mechanics (e.g., capitalization) should be taught when the need arises, not as isolated skills; (b) mechanics are never as important as the composition itself; and (c) mechanics should be explained as needed and children should be convinced of their importance and encouraged to use them again and again in meaningful ways until their use becomes second nature.

An article by Boutwell (12) and two pieces by Dawson (19; 20) were written in the same spirit. Among Dawson's (20) points:

1. Concentrate on a few major items each school year.

2. Work on the errors one at a time. Devote one full lesson and then repeat for five-minute intervals regularly. Aim at thorough mastery. Review all year but after a month's concentration on one error, begin on another one.

3. Suit the type of exercise to the stage of learning.

4. Emphasize oral drill. Work in small groups or individually, but children must say the words with their own tongues.

5. Use a positive, not negative, approach. Set up situations in which children must respond with correct usage.

6. Give written practice on items of written usage. One effective way to practice punctuation and capitalization is dictation.

7. Except for errors common to most of the class, individualize lessons.

How Shall We Approach Instruction in Grammar?

While the controversy over "formal" or "methodical" instruction in grammar versus the "functional" or "usage" approach *appears* to have continued over the past five to eight years, careful reading of the literature fails to disclose as wide a schism as one might at first think. In other words, much of the heat in the arguments is semantic.

Specifically, the "formalist" sometimes assails "functionalist" practices of the most *doubtful* nature as *typical* of *all* functionalist practice, and vice versa. As Adler and Mayer—in a different context—recently phrased it, "The traditionalist accuses the modernist of assuming that the world began yesterday, and the modernist accuses the traditionalist of assuming that it ended a century ago." [1] *Truth* apparently lies somewhere between most extreme positions!

Conflicting viewpoints. Literature of the past few years presents few if any articles that suggest that good grammar is unimportant. Nor does any

[1] Mortimer J. Adler and Milton Mayer. *The Revolution in Education.* Chicago: The University of Chicago Press, 1958. p. 105.

88

body of writings support rote or memoritor learning of formal rules of grammar without reference to meaning. Essentially, the differences in opinion arise between persons who contend that "grammar should be taught" and those who point out that "Premature, formal work in grammar is not an effective way of improving usage." These positions are not true opposites since neither group denies the importance of children and youth's knowing the forms and structure of words or their customary arrangement in phrases and sentences.

Among representative writers who appear to side or sympathize with a thoroughgoing emphasis on grammar are Binney (9), Jandoli (29), Miller (42), and Lessen (33). No one among them suggests a return to 1890 drills, however. Rather, they urge that a better job be done. Proponents of "functional" or "use" approaches, as urged by Symonds (64) or Frogner (24) as far back as the early 1930s, include Asker (5), DeBoer (22), and a Baltimore Public Schools committee (7).

Educators need to recognize that there is a general consensus as to the importance of good usage and that disagreement as to the means of improving usage is by no means violent. This is apparent from data in the next two sections pertaining to trends in practice and research findings.

Current Trends and Recent Research

Trends in instruction. Strom (61) has provided a useful review of the literature for more than 50 years prior to 1960 as it related to knowledge of grammar and ability to communicate. Her 23-page booklet carefully traced trends in viewpoints and concluded with a 77-item bibliography.

Pooley has contributed three helpful publications. One of these was an analysis of courses of study which indicated that structural grammar was still widely taught (47:41-48). Two other Pooley articles were succinct statements of his views on the ineffectuality of overstressing grammar during the early grades (48) and his answer to the question, "What grammar shall I teach?" (49). An able scholar, Pooley is not "anti-grammar," but he urged restraint in introducing rote or formal instruction to improve speaking and composition during children's earlier years in school.

A 1960 questionnaire study made by Alva (2) in the high schools of California led him to the conclusion that structural grammar was generally taught throughout the year and was slowly becoming the object of greater emphasis. Alva's (1) doctoral study presented more detailed information than the article cited above. In a study of college placement tests, Litzey (34) reported increasing stress on English usage but less interest in mastery of technical grammatical terms.

Recent research. Research other than "trend studies" (such as those cited above) that pertained to grammar was published by a variety of authors. Otterman (45) worked with 585 seventh graders to evaluate the systematic study of prefixes and word-roots. The experimental group in her controlled study was given daily prefix and word-root instruction. Results were encouraging with respect to spelling and prefix and root-word recall, but improvements in reading speed and comprehension and in vocabulary were not significant.

Walter (66) reported on developmental stages in the written sentences of children in New South Wales, Australia, identifying the order of emergence of parts of speech and constructions. In an Oregon high school, Kraus (31) introduced three approaches to the teaching of sentence structure to compare their effectiveness. This approach, Kraus said, linked to the use of literature and to weekly themes as a basis of instruction proved to be superior to the more conventional methods. Brown (13) arrived at the amusing conclusion that ". . . the nouns used by young [three- to five-year-old] English-speaking children were more reliably the names of things and their verbs more reliably the names of actions than in the case for nouns and verbs used by English-speaking adults." Adults—watch your language!

Brown and Berko (14) studied word association and the acquisition of grammar by primary level Massachusetts youngsters and deduced " . . . the formal change in word association and the ability to make correct grammatical use of new words are two manifestations of the child's developing appreciation of English syntax." Walderman and Triggs (65) reported on word attack skills tests; Mallis (36) described procedures in teaching grammar more effectively; and McElroy (39) claimed success at the secondary level in teaching grammar in conjunction with literature.

Concise information regarding the importance of prefixes and suffixes was provided by Fitzgerald (23) who stated that 25 percent of our language is made up of prefix-suffix derivatives. In a doctoral study, Pippert (46) examined the prediction of the correctness of post high school written language performance. His Wisconsin secondary school graduates were studied over a five-year period with respect to the mechanics of their written language.

Also of interest was Strom's (60) approach to the question of whether or not a knowledge of grammar functions in reading. Little relationship existed, she found, between 327 sophomore pupils' comprehension of selected poetry and prose and their ability to classify elements of grammar and syntax in the sentences of the literary passages. Exceptions to this generalization were four groups of pupils from a laboratory school.

On the whole, the research reviewed did not suggest that major changes in current practices were under way, although numerous interesting pieces of disparate information were added to present knowledge.

90

References to Semantics and Linguistics

The professional interest of teachers and the increase in articles during the late 1950s combine in reflecting the increased emphasis on linguistics and semantics. Among general commentators was Boutwell (11) who noted that "The new grammar, based on the new science of linguistics, deserves a cordial welcome." Thoughtful and provocative articles also were written by Simonini (55), Long (35), Williams (68), and Anderson (3). Among them they provide the interested reader with an overview of current opinion. Simonini, for example, clarified the meaning of linguistics, advocated major emphasis on linguistics in teacher education, and suggested appropriate university level course work. Long defined the conflict between the "new linguists" and the "traditional grammarians," and Anderson discussed structural linguistics.

Kaufman (30) wrote on semantics, and Weaver (67) contributed a recondite study of the semantic distance between twelfth grade students and their teachers and its effect upon learning. Other research reports by Senatore (54), who discussed his work with a "sentence pattern method" of studying English sentences, and by Malmstrom are worth attention.

Malmstrom made a study (38) which compared information from a linguistic atlas and various textbook pronouncements on current American usage. She reviewed 57 usage items in grades three, six, and eight as they appeared in 2,000 textbooks in English that were published over a 15-year period and made direct use of 312 of these publications in her work.

In her 1959 summary report in the *English Journal,* Malmstrom (37) concluded that there was no set standard of usage. Rather it varied with dialect and area and any evaluation of usage was necessarily influenced or governed by five considerations: social elements, the particular situation, regional factors, time elements, and methodological considerations. Detailed data on which Malmstrom based her article are preserved in her University of Minnesota thesis (38).

Grammar and Teacher Education

A few authors recently have been concerned with grammar and usage in publications with a bearing on teacher education. Smith (57) and Conlin (17), in the same issue of an influential journal, respectively discussed (a) the merits of grammar as a part of language arts instruction and (b) the view that traditional grammar should be revised rather than supplanted by application of principles derived from structural linguistics. Points made by Conlin with relevance for teacher preparation included:

1. Teachers should have knowledge of phonemics as a basis for teaching reading, spelling, and sentence structure.

2. Teachers should be familiar with modern studies in usage.

3. Teachers should know the essential differences between the spoken language, and its derived form, writing.

4. Teachers should be familiar with the structure of the language, basic forms, patterns of speech, and necessity for objective description and analysis of language based on form.

5. Teachers should understand the nature of language and language habits and help students learn to observe language.

6. Teachers should have knowledge of the nature of meaning and its relation to the problem of listening and interpretation.

A questionnaire was sent to chairmen of college English departments by Slothower (56) in his effort to ascertain the preparation being given prospective teachers of secondary level English. According to the 360 chairmen who responded:

1. The study of grammar was stressed in required courses.

2. Emphasis was placed on improving usage.

3. An attempt was being made to broaden course work to include attention to psychological and social dimensions of language.

4. About half of the colleges gave little heed to structural grammar.

5. Those English departments that were not doing much with structural grammar usually did not contemplate changing their policies.

Variations in teacher preparation were reflected in Womack's (69) study of teachers' attitudes toward current usage. A 39 percent return from 45 states and the District of Columbia revealed decidedly diverse teacher opinion on 50 debatable items of usage in both formal and informal speech and writing. Teachers' attitudes were affected by two kinds of experience: *academic,* as revealed by background of course work and familiarity with important publications in language study; and *environmental and social,* including size of community in which the teacher taught, years of teaching experience, and the grade level at which he taught.

Criger (18) expressed criticism of the preparation of teachers particularly with respect to what he deemed an emphasis on literature in colleges at the expense of grammar.

Mostly on the Lighter Side

A few articles, either entertaining or instructive or both, serve to round out the résumé of opinion and data in this section. Bryant (15) sympathetically commented on the role of the double negative, and Holbrook (28) amused himself and others in the *New Yorker* with an essay on the use of the apostrophe in such expressions as "fish 'n chips" which he had schooled himself to accept with fortitude!

A plea for using phonetic signs with written English was made by Chevallier (16) in the *London Times;* Bolinger (10) discussed the relative importance of grammatical items; and Ong (44) provided a pleasant concluding point relevant to grammar—the point that communication is rooted not in things but in human beings. Like these beings, language, including the system of word arrangements and structure we call grammar, is so seemingly sentient with a mysterious inner life that it radically resists being structured at all.

Summary

A summary that is brief, indeed, seems in order. In a few phrases, the world of Aelius Donatus, the fourth century Roman who did much to codify formal grammar in a design that endured for over a thousand years after his death, has gone beyond the point of no return.

Few any longer defend meaningless, rote rule-learning, and we seem to be over the threshold of a more businesslike but also more flexible approach to grammar and usage.

Bibliography

1. ALVA, CHARLES A. "Descriptive Grammar in the Teaching of English: A Survey of Its Extent, Use, and Status in the Public High Schools of California." Unpublished doctoral thesis. Stanford, California: Stanford University, 1959. 197 p.

2. ALVA, CHARLES A. "Structural Grammar in California High Schools." *English Journal* 49:606-11; December 1960.

3. ANDERSON, W. L. "Structural Linguistics: Some Implications and Applications." *English Journal* 46:410-18; October 1957.

4. APPLEGATE, MAUREE. "Language Arts: To Make Mechanics Serve Ideas." *Grade Teacher* 74:38+; June 1957.

5. ASKER, WILLIAM. "Does Knowledge of Formal Grammar Function?" *School and Society,* January 1923. p. 109-11.

6. BAKER, ORVILLE, and ROBERT H. DeZONIA. "Achievement in Mechanics in Freshman English." *College English* 21:389-91; April 1960.

7. BALTIMORE BULLETIN OF EDUCATION. "Does Teaching Grammar Help Children To Write and Speak Better?" *Baltimore Bulletin of Education* 36:25-29; April 1959.

8. BATEMAN, DONALD R. "More Mature Writing Through a Better Understanding of Language Structure." *English Journal* 50:457-60, 468; October 1961.

9. BINNEY, JAMES. "Short Report Concerning Grammar." *Education* 76:472-77; April 1956.

10. BOLINGER, DWIGHT L. "The Relative Importance of Grammatical Items." *Hispania* 38:261-64; September 1955.

11. BOUTWELL, WILLIAM D. "What's Happening in Education? New Method of Teaching Grammar?" *National Parent-Teacher* 52:11; September 1957.

12. BOUTWELL, WILLIAM D. "What's Happening in Education?" *National Parent-Teacher* 51:15-16; April 1957.

13. BROWN, ROGER W. "Linguistic Determinism and the Parts of Speech." *Journal of Abnormal and Social Psychology* 55:1-5; 1957.

14. BROWN, ROGER W., and JEAN BERKO. "Word Association and the Acquisition of Grammar." *Child Development* 31:1-14; March 1960.

15. BRYANT, M. M. "Double Negative." *College English* 19:229; February 1958.

16. CHEVALLIER, J. M. "English for External Use: Phonetic Signs in Writing." *London Times Educational Supplement,* March 12, 1954. p. 236.

17. CONLIN, D. A. "Can Traditional Grammar Be Modernized?" *English Journal* 47:189-94; April 1958.

18. CRIGER, C. G. "Teachers of English Versus Teachers of Literature." *California Journal of Secondary Education* 35:502-504; December 1960.

19. DAWSON, MILDRED A. "Help Your Children Get Sentence Sense." *Instructor* 68:53+; November 1958.

20. DAWSON, MILDRED A. "If Your Pupils Always Use Good English." *Instructor* 68:24+; October 1958.

21. DAY, JOSEPH E. "English Fundamentals Class Nets Gain." *Overview* 1:68; February 1960.

22. DEBOER, JOHN. "Grammar in Language Teaching." *Elementary English* 36:413-21; October 1959.

23. FITZGERALD, JAMES A. "Prefixes in Child Writing." *Elementary English* 36:576-80; December 1959.

24. FROGNER, ELLEN. "Grammar Approach Versus Thought Approach in Teaching Sentence Structure." *English Journal* 28:518-26; 1939.

25. GROFF, PATRICK J. "Effect of Knowledge of Parts of Speech on College Entrance Examinations in California." *California Journal of Secondary Education* 35:415-17; November 1960.

26. GROFF, PATRICK J. "Is Knowledge of Parts of Speech Necessary?" *English Journal* 50:413-15; September 1961.

27. HEWITT, E. A. "Performance in English Language at O Level of a Sample of University Students." *British Journal of Educational Psychology* 30:40-46; February 1960.

28. HOLBROOK, WEARE. "The Ampers 'N.'" *New Yorker* 31:134-35; October 1, 1955.

29. JANDOLI, RUSSELL. "What's Happening to English?" *Catholic World* 178:426-31; March 1954.

30. KAUFMAN, HELEN J. "The Semantic Differential: A Critical Appraisal." *Public Opinion Quarterly* 23:437-38; Fall 1959.

31. KRAUS, SILVY ASHER. "A Comparison of Three Methods of Teaching Sentence Structure." *Dissertation Abstracts* 19:2808; 1959.

32. KUNHART, WILLIAM E., and LIONEL R. OLSEN. "An Analysis of Test Scores and Grades for Predicting Success of College Students in English Composition." *Journal of Educational Research* 53:79; October 1959.

33. LESSEN, SHELDON. "Grammar Has a Place in the Classroom." *English Journal* 43:260-61; May 1954.

34. LITZEY, DAVID M. "Trends in College Placement Tests in Freshman English." *English Journal* 45:250-56; May 1956.

35. LONG, R. B. "Words, Meanings, Literacy, and Grammar." *English Journal* 47:195-99; April 1958.

36. MALLIS, J. "Experiment with the New Grammar." *English Journal* 46:425-27; October 1957.

37. MALMSTROM, JEAN. "Linguistic Atlas Findings Versus Textbook Pronouncements on Current American Usage." *English Journal* 48:191-98; April 1959.

38. MALMSTROM, JEAN. "A Study of the Validity of Textbook Statements About Certain Controversial Grammatical Items in the Light of Evidence from the Linguistic Atlas." *Dissertation Abstracts* 19:1306-1307; No. 6; 1958.

39. McELROY, M. D. "Let Grammar Grow." *English Journal* 43:151-53; March 1954.

40. McKEY, ELEANOR F. "The Standardized Test: Are Improvements Needed?" *English Journal* 49:35-37; January 1960.

41. MEADE, RICHARD A. "Who Can Learn Grammar?" *English Journal* 50:87-92; February 1961.

42. MILLER, C. G. "Is Correct English Worth the Price?" *Clearing House* 32:135-36; November 1957.

43. ODOM, ROBERT R. "Sequence and Grade Placement of Capitalization Skills." *Elementary English* 38:118-21; February 1961.

44. ONG, W. J. "Grammar Today: Structure in a Vocal World." *Quarterly Journal of Speech* 43:399-407; December 1957.

45. OTTERMAN, LOIS M. "The Value of Teaching Prefixes and Word Roots." *Journal of Educational Research* 48:611-14; April 1955.

46. PIPPERT, RALPH REINHARD. "The Prediction of the Correctness of Post-High School Written Language Performance." Unpublished doctoral thesis. Madison: University of Wisconsin, 1959. 119 p.

47. POOLEY, ROBERT C. "The Evidence from Courses of Study." *Teaching English Grammar*. New York: Appleton-Century-Crofts, 1957. p. 41-48.

48. POOLEY, ROBERT C. "Grammar in the Grades?" *NEA Journal* 47:422; September 1958.

49. POOLEY, ROBERT C. "What Grammar Shall I Teach?" *English Journal* 47:327-33; September 1958.

50. REMONDINO, C. "Factorial Analysis of the Evaluation of Scholastic Compositions in the Mother Tongue." *British Journal of Educational Psychology* 29:242-51; November 1959.

51. ROBINSON, NORA. "The Relation Between Knowledge of English Grammar and Ability in English Composition." *British Journal of Educational Psychology* 30:184-86; Part II; June 1960.

52. SCHUSTER, EDGAR H. "How Good Is the New Grammar?" *English Journal* 50:392-97; September 1961.

53. SEARLERS, JOHN R., and G. ROBERT CARLSEN. "Language, Grammar, and Composition." *Encyclopedia of Educational Research*. American Educational Research Association. New York: The Macmillan Company, 1960. p. 454-70.

54. SENATORE, JOHN J. "SVO: A Key to Clearer Language Teaching." *English Journal* 46:419-24; October 1957.

55. SIMONINI, RINALDO C. "Linguistics in the English Curriculum." *College English* 19:163-65; January 1958.

56. SLOTHOWER, WILLIAM R. "English-Language Preparation Required of Prospective Teachers of High School English in American Colleges and Universities." Unpublished doctoral thesis. Urbana: University of Illinois, 1959. 157 p.

57. SMITH, H. L., JR. "Teacher and the World of English." *English Journal* 47:181-88; April 1958.

58. STRICKLAND, RUTH G. "Evaluating Children's Composition." *Elementary English* 37:321-31; May 1960.

59. STROM, INGRID M. "Do Grammar Drills Help Writing Skills?" *NEA Journal* 49:25; December 1960.

60. STROM, INGRID M. "Does Knowledge of Grammar Improve Reading?" *English Journal* 45:129-33; March 1956.

61. STROM, INGRID M. *Research in Grammar and Usage and Its Implications for Teacher Writings.* Bulletin of the School of Education, Vol. 36, No. 5. Bloomington: Indiana University, 1960. 23 p.

62. STROM, INGRID M. "Research in Teaching Grammar and Usage." *Education Digest* 26:50-52; January 1961.

63. SUGGE, LENA REDDICK. "Structural Grammar Versus Traditional Grammar in Influencing Writing." *English Journal* 50:174-78; March 1961.

64. SYMONDS, PERCIVAL M. "Practice Versus Grammar in the Learning of Correct English Usage." *Journal of Educational Psychology,* February 1931. p. 81-96.

65. WALDERMAN, J., and F. O. TRIGGS. "Measurement of Word Attack Skills." *Elementary English* 35:459-63; November 1958.

66. WALTER, JENA. "A Study of the Written Sentence Construction of a Group of Profoundly Deaf Children." *American Annals of the Deaf* 100:235-52; 1955.

67. WEAVER, CARL H. "Semantic Distance Between Students and Teachers and Its Effect upon Learning." *Speech Monographs* 26:273-81; November 1959.

68. WILLIAMS, ROBERT D. "Linguistics and Grammar." *English Journal* 48:388-92; October 1959.

69. WOMACK, THURSTON. "Teacher's Attitudes Toward Current Usage." *English Journal* 48:186-90; April 1959.

70. ZEIGLER, MARTIN L., and LOUIS M. HERMAN. "A Study of the Effectiveness of a Summer Remedial Course in English for College Freshmen." *Journal of Educational Research* 53:76-78; October 1959.

Chapter Seven

Literature
for Children and Youth

WRITINGS and research related to the role and importance of literature in the education of children and youth have become somewhat more abundant than they were a decade ago. Teachers who enjoy sharing literature with children will find many who urge them to continue. Those interested in what books to choose also will find more advice available.

Overviews and Commentaries

"General interest" items. Jacobs (21), in his usual pleasant and convincing style, has pointed to the values of literature, as has Duff (16). Calitri (7) wrote of the importance of reading deeply in good books, while James S. Smith (31) criticized superficial thinking in the selection of materials by teachers (e.g., "Is it on the list?" or "What 'unit' can I use this with?"). Dora V. Smith (30) summarized her impressions of children's books around the world after completing an extensive overseas trip.

Williams (34) concerned herself with the importance of improving pupils' taste in selecting prose fiction, and Squire (32) dealt with assaying "literacy in literature." Early (17) wrote thoughtfully on stages of growth in literary appreciation, while Cook (13:136-37) presented criteria for selecting and evaluating literary materials:

1. Each material chosen must have some teaching value—a value that can be named, even though it cannot be scientifically measured.

2. Materials should be chosen in relation to a plan for continuous development.

3. Materials in literature should be selected with due regard to the maturity level for which they are intended.

Arbuthnot (3), long known for her devotion to children's literature, wrote an inspired article on "books that open windows," while Darling (14) treated bibliotherapy as a means of diminishing emotional problems.

Research Studies

Research related to literature for children and youth often was concerned with the question of story preferences. The research studies reviewed were varied in their foci.

What are the literary preferences of children? Landau (23) found that 120 children and 25 experts in literature closely agreed on what were and were not amusing or entertaining books in a study that must have provided much comfort to the adults involved. Another study comparing adult and child preferences in juvenile literature was done by Jefferson (22). The favorite tales of boys and girls and the favorites of their respective parents were investigated. Distinct sex differences were noted, and parents proved to be quite adept in judging what their individual children liked.

Avegno (4), Browman and Templin (6), Vandament and Thalman (33), and Rudman (28) were among research workers who made inquiries into children's literary interests. A large sample was involved in all except the Browman-Templin study, which was longitudinal and contrasted stories recommended for young children in the 1920s and in the 1950s. While data from the other three inquiries are too detailed to reproduce, an excerpt is made from each:

Avegno: The six poems best-liked by fourth to sixth graders out of 130 written prior to 1900 were "The Owl and the Pussy Cat," "He Thought He Saw," "The Table and the Chair," "The Monkeys and the Crocodile," "Little Billee," and "My Shadow."

Vandament-Thalman: Story books were more popular than comic books which in turn were more popular than magazines in a group of 1,034 Illinois sixth and tenth graders.

Rudman: As children in a 270-community sample moved through the grades, their interest in mystery stories increased and it decreased in cowboy stories and fairy tales.

Amsden (2) worked in 1960 with 60 preschool children to determine their responses to color and style in illustrations. Her findings (e.g., dark shades in illustrations are significantly preferred to bright, saturated colors) should be of particular interest to nursery-kindergarten level teachers. Slover (29) explored comic books as a possible threat to regular story books in the fourth grade and found that a small majority of youngsters preferred comics but also were enjoying "good" books. Those fourth graders who read best or had the higher I.Q.s already were leaving the "comic book stage" at this grade level.

Collier and Gaier made four reports between 1958 and 1960 on literary preferences. In the first of these (10), 264 college students were asked to recall and summarize favorite childhood tales. One result was that ". . . types of stories preferred and the manner of reporting them appear

98

to reflect cultural and possibly biological, sex-role expectancies." A second 1958 study (12) revealed the preferred childhood stories of 184 college women: *Cinderella* and *Snow White* were favorite fairy tales; *Little Women* and the *Bobbsey Twins* were most popular as general fiction; *Black Beauty* ran first among animal stories.

A third Collier-Gaier (11) report in 1959 listed 80 undergraduate male preferences as to heroes in remembered childhood tales. Tom Sawyer and Robinson Crusoe were top contenders. The most recent of their articles (1960) was a Gaier-Collier (18) statement comparing latency-stage story preferences of 199 American and 120 Finnish children of fourth and fifth grade age. No single tale was "most favored" by either group, but the children preferred fiction with exciting, narrative passages, and the recency of a child's contact with a story influenced stated preference. Sex differences in story preference were distinct.

Miscellaneous Research with a Bearing on Children's Literature

Literature and the adolescent. The history of books designed for young adolescents was succintly reviewed by Alm (1) and Carpenter (9) who noted that the fictional teen-age heroes in recent novels were identified with the problems of an adolescent civilization.

Hand (19) concerned himself with modern novels in high school English classes in Michigan and recorded both practices and teachers' opinions as to their roles. Sample finding: modern novels are used much more frequently for outside reading than for classroom instruction. Hand (20) also dealt with the problem of the high school English teacher in studying modern novels which deal with sex and suggested several questions for the teacher to answer in making selections of teen-age reading material.

Trends in the teaching of literature in senior high school, as reflected in professional journals since 1911, were surveyed by Moulton (25). Baker (5) studied simplified (i.e., rewritten) classics. Fifty-two adaptations were scanned and found to vary a good bit in their altered forms. *Ivanhoe,* for instance, rated 12.1 in difficulty when the Yoakum formula was applied to the original text. Six simplified versions of the Sir Walter Scott novel ranged from 4.3 to 10.8 with the same formula. Patently, blanket condemnation or approval for reworked classics is unwise—especially when "story detail retention" also was found to vary from 3 percent to 41 percent.

Too varied to classify. The spontaneous responses of 2,500 kindergartners who had just listened to stories read to them by their teachers were preserved by Cappa (8). The most common response—desiring to look at the book—occurred in 38.2 percent of the cases. Other responses included drawing, painting, dramatic play, and so on. Delaney (15) described a Junior Great Books program for grades five through twelve, while Opie and Opie (26) collected data for five years in the United Kingdom prior to reporting on the lore and language of school children, including their made-up verses.

Mahar and Fisher (24) compiled a useful list of library resource materials, and Otto and Flournoy (27) did a thorough job on "Printed Materials" for a research journal.

Summary

By its very nature, the field of children's literature (considered as separate and distinct from the realm of reading) seems to afford relatively few avenues for research. Opinion studies, studies of literary preferences, historical studies, and the like were among those most widely done.

Because of the delight that good books bring the reader and because of the personal nature of the enjoyment of good literature, perhaps we can afford an area in the language arts field that largely has escaped the researchers' controls and dissections!

Bibliography

1. ALM, R. S. "Development of Literature for Adolescents." *School Review* 64:172-77; April 1956.
2. AMSDEN, RUTH. "Children's Preferences in Picture Story Book Variables." *Journal of Educational Research* 53:309-12; April 1960.
3. ARBUTHNOT, MAY HILL. "Books That Open Windows." *Childhood Education* 36:263-66; February 1960.
4. AVEGNO, SYLVIA T. "Intermediate-Grade Children's Choices of Poetry." *Elementary English* 33:428-32; November 1956.
5. BAKER, IRVING DUMOND. "An Evaluation of the Simplified Classics." Unpublished doctoral thesis. Pittsburgh: University of Pittsburgh, 1960. 122 p.
6. BROWMAN, MARGARET T., and MILDRED C. TEMPLIN. "Stories for Younger Children in 1927-29 and in 1952-55." *Elementary School Journal* 59:324-27; March 1959.
7. CALITRI, CHARLES. "Macbeth and the Reluctant Reader." *English Journal* 48:254-61; May 1959.
8. CAPPA, D. "Kindergarten Children's Spontaneous Responses to Story Books Read by the Teacher." *Journal of Educational Research* 52:75; October 1958.
9. CARPENTER, FREDERICK L. "The Adolescent in American Fiction." *English Journal* 46:313-19; September 1957.
10. COLLIER, MARY J., and EUGENE L. GAIER. "Adult Reactions to Preferred Childhood Stories." *Child Development* 29:97-103; March 1958.
11. COLLIER, MARY J., and EUGENE L. GAIER. "The Hero in the Preferred Childhood Stories of College Men." *American Imago* 16:17-194; Summer 1959.
12. COLLIER, MARY J., and EUGENE L. GAIER. "Preferred Childhood Stories of College Women." *American Imago* 15:401-10; Winter 1958.

13. COOK, LUELLA B. "Criteria for Selecting and Evaluating Reading Materials in Literature." *Materials in Reading*. H. M. Robinson, editor. Supplementary Educational Monographs, No. 86. Chicago: University of Chicago Press, December 1957. p. 133-37.

14. DARLING, RICHARD L. "Mental Hygiene and Books: Bibliotherapy as Used with Children and Adolescents." *Wilson Library Bulletin* 32:293-96; December 1957.

15. DELANEY, W. P. "Junior Great Books Program." *Catholic School Journal* 60:27-28; February 1960.

16. DUFF, ANNIS. "Literary Heritage of Childhood." *Wilson Library Bulletin* 33:563-70; April 1959.

17. EARLY, MARGARET J. "Stages of Growth in Literary Appreciation." *English Journal* 49:161-67; March 1960.

18. GAIER, EUGENE L., and MARY J. COLLIER. "The Latency-Stage Story Preferences of American and Finnish Children." *Child Development* 31:431-51; September 1960.

19. HAND, HARRY E. "Modern Novels in Senior High School English: A Study Concerning Practices and Opinions of Teachers of High School English in the State of Michigan." *Dissertation Abstracts* 19:3304; No. 12; 1959.

20. HAND, HARRY E. "Sex in the Modern Novel: A Teaching Problem." *English Journal* 48:473-76; November 1959.

21. JACOBS, LELAND B. "Children Need Literature." *Elementary English* 32:12-16; January 1955.

22. JEFFERSON, BENJAMIN F. "Some Relationships Between Parents' and Children's Preferences in Juvenile Literature." *Elementary School Journal* 58:212-18; January 1958.

23. LANDAU, ELLIOTT D. "The Children and the Experts Agree." *Elementary English* 34:561-63; December 1957.

24. MAHAR, M. H., and G. B. FISHER. "School Library Materials." *School Life* 41:20-21; January 1959.

25. MOULTON, DOROTHY E. "The Teaching of Literature in the Senior High School: A Historical and Critical Study of Recent Trends Based upon an Analysis of Selected Professional Publications, 1911-1955." *Dissertation Abstracts* 20:1692; November 1959.

26. OPIE, I., and P. OPIE. "Lore and Language of School Children." *Library Journal* 85:1981-83; May 15, 1960.

27. OTTO, HENRY J., and FRANCES FLOURNOY. "Printed Materials." *Review of Educational Research* 26:115-24; April 1956.

28. RUDMAN, HERBERT C. "The Informational Needs and Reading Interests of Children in Grades IV Through VIII." *Elementary School Journal* 55:502-12; May 1955.

29. SLOVER, VERA. "Comic Books Versus Story Books." *Elementary English* 36:319-22; May 1959.

30. SMITH, DORA V. "Children's Books Around the World." *Elementary English* 35:81-92; February 1958.

31. SMITH, JAMES S. "Blind Alleys in Children's Literature." *Elementary English* 36:223-25; April 1959.

32. SQUIRE, JAMES R. "Literacy and Literature." *English Journal* 49:154-60; March 1960.

33. VANDAMENT, WILLIAM E., and W. A. THALMAN. "An Investigation into the Reading Interests of Children." *Journal of Educational Research* 49:467-70; February 1956.

34. WILLIAMS, ELIZABETH. "Teaching Judgment of Prose Fiction." *English Journal* 47:495-99; November 1958.

Chapter Eight

"Listen, My Children, and You Shall Hear . . ."

IN RECENT years many teachers have become aware of the importance of listening in the learning process. In other words, *listening* is now construed to signify much more than seeing that children "pay attention" in the classroom. As a result, a more methodical approach to helping children acquire listening skills has become increasingly common in American elementary and secondary schools. In the literature one finds frequent mention of the importance of "auding" in language arts programs—a term which has been defined by Caffrey (12:121) as ". . . the process of hearing, listening to, recognizing, and interpreting or comprehending spoken language."

Children spend a great deal of time during the school day receiving oral messages from many sources—the classroom teacher, special teachers, classmates, parents, neighbors, radio, television, and so forth. Despite the extent of this aural experience, we still do not fully understand how they have interpreted what they heard or thought they heard. In listening, as in other areas of the language arts such as speaking, reading, and writing, one's previous background of experience is the source or basis for interpreting a symbol or sound or other medium of communication. To illustrate: two musicians, a violinist and a cellist, were walking along the streets of London and conversing about their work as members of a symphony orchestra. While they were exchanging opinions as to the effectiveness of their most recent performance, a bell was being raised with a block and tackle in the tower of a church in the immediate vicinity. Suddenly the tackle broke, and the bell fell with a resounding clang.

"What was that?" exclaimed the violinist in alarm. "F sharp," replied the cellist.

Each of us, as the story points out, hears, comprehends, and interprets in the light of his unique background. We are the product of our experiences —they affect what we read, write, say, and *hear*.

Surveys of Research

A review of experimental research studies in the area of hearing, its importance in learning situations, and its comparison to methods of visual learning was completed by Witty and Sizemore (61) in 1958. Other reviews of research were published in the *Review of Educational Research* by Lewis (40) in 1958 and Duker (20) in 1961. The reader may well want to review the many studies of listening presented in these three articles.

Goals for Listening

In an article published in 1961, Duker (19) listed ten desirable qualities of a good listener. He stressed the need for schools to develop the following qualities in their programs: (a) listeners who listen, (b) selective listening, (c) skillful listening, (d) critical listening, (e) courteous listening, (f) attentive listening, (g) retentive listening, (h) curious listening, (i) reactive listening, and (j) reflective listening. Furness (25) surveyed the literature related to listening and listed the objectives and effects of a listening program which current writings implied. Another article which suggested goals for listening, some desirable aspects of a listening environment, and some principles of learning to be observed in cultivating listening ability was written by Lewis (39).

What is listening? Stressing the fact that listening must be done for a purpose in an atmosphere conducive to listening, Furness (24) discussed proportion, purpose, and process in listening. Schwartz (52) talked about listening and ways the teacher can help children learn to listen. Ten components of effective listening were provided by Nichols (49):

1. Previous experience with difficult material
2. Interest in the topic at hand
3. Adjustment to the speaker
4. Energy expenditure of the listener
5. Adjustment to the abnormal listening situation
6. Adjustment to emotion-laden words
7. Adjusting to emotion-rousing points
8. Recognition of central ideas
9. Utilization of notes
10. Reconciliation of thought speed and speech speed.

General Suggestions for Teachers

Many writers feel that students can be taught to listen and that training in this skill often will increase the general academic success of children and youth. Previous research has indicated that children, particularly in the early years of school, spend a great part of the day listening. Because of this, Kelley (36) emphasized the point that principles of good listening should be taught in the kindergarten and primary grades. Her article incorporated ideas and activities suitable for this age group. Concerned also with the beginning school child, Snider (55) reported on her study on the attitudes of kindergarten children toward specially prepared story materials. To determine the importance of listening skill as it related to visual skills, King (37) studied children in nine primary schools in England. He found there was, among other things, a marked tendency for boys to do better than girls on some of the oral tests of listening with practical content.

Both Pratt (51) and Sister M. K. Hollow (53) reported investigations concerned with intermediate age elementary school children. These writers' findings indicated that reading ability and intelligence had some kinship with listening ability. Teachers of this nine-to-twelve-year-old age group will be interested in Hampleman's (29) work which compared the listening and reading comprehension ability of fourth and sixth grade pupils. Dow (18) also wrote about the teaching of reading and listening and provided a list of comprehension factors common to both reading and listening.

The "approval factor" in listening is important, according to Nichols and Cashman (50), who warn adults to be careful how they listen before children because children tend to imitate both good and bad habits. Listening ability and human interest concerned Cartier (14), who studied over 100 tenth grade students in California to determine the effect of listening ability on the average listener.

General articles designed, among other things, to stimulate interest in listening, to increase literary appreciation, and to improve oral communication were written by Smith (54), Forbes (22), Canfield (13), and Barbe and Myers (1). A number of excellent suggestions for improving functional listening-learning situations are included in these reports.

College instructors in particular should be interested in Markgraf's (45) survey of listening pedagogy in American teacher-education institutions. Questionnaires were returned by 406 institutions in an attempt to determine:

1. If listening is being taught in teacher-education institutions

2. If material concerning the teaching of listening is being taught

3. If prospective teachers have opportunities to observe the teaching of listening and if they are given opportunities to teach listening

4. What are the attitudes of professors of educational methods courses toward the teaching of listening.

More specific reports. The relationship between listening ability and readability was investigated by Harwood (31) who studied children's

104

written and spoken language at various levels of difficulty. He also has reported on his study to determine (a) whether listening ability of the language samples was affected significantly by rate of presentation, (b) whether the effects of such a presentation were consistent at the different rates, and (c) whether readability was a consistent predictor of listening ability at different rates (30). Another interesting report is one which presents a résumé of an experiment conducted by Moyer (48) to find possible answers to questions which have arisen concerning the improvement of English usage through ear-training. Another person investigating a major component of oral presentation, namely speaking rate, was Goodman-Malamuth (26) who studied the possible effects of speaking rate upon the understanding of the materials heard at various levels of measured difficulty.

Edgar (21) reported that his research findings suggest that the listening ability of pupils in grades four, five, and six can be improved by any of the four specific methods of training he describes in his study. Stressing the need to develop the "listening ear," Fulton (23) prepared an article that suggested the importance of language laboratories in fostering listening skills.

Listening and Other Areas of the Curriculum

Interest in the relationship between various areas of the curriculum or subjects and listening skills has been high both among teachers and researchers. In comparing the size and nature of reading and listening vocabularies of 211 secondary school students, Kegler (35) found a close relationship between vocabulary and grade level, intelligence, and reading ability. In an analogous inquiry, Still (57) indicated that his work pointed to the general conclusion that there is a positive relationship between listening and high school grades. In addition, Caffery (11), at the secondary school level, attempted to make a precise estimate of the nature of auding ability and its relation to reading, writing, and spelling.

Beery (4), after studying children in elementary and secondary schools and colleges, advised the reader of the interrelationships found among speaking, listening, reading, and writing. Children in several elementary schools in Indiana were studied by Marten (46) to determine the relationship between expressed interests and listening skills of children in the sixth grade.

Both Hosey (33) and Crosby (16) concerned themselves with speaking and listening. Hosey presented techniques to help students speak more correctly as an outcome of listening, while Crosby's interesting and informative article presented social situations and other situations which help to develop listening and speaking skills for a purpose.

At the college level. The improvement of listening skills has concerned research workers not only at the elementary and secondary levels but in the colleges as well. For example, Westover (59) compared listening and reading ability as a means of testing students when he investigated their ability to answer objective questions read to them in comparison with their ability to answer similar questions that they read themselves. Black (6), in an inquiry of interest to teachers, studied the length of sentences and how this affects the listener's identification of the words in the sentence. He also took into account the amount of environmental noise in which the sentences were heard.

The performance of college students seems to indicate, according to Brown (8), that, if the listener will give attention to the preparatory remarks a speaker may make, this will help in the retention of what the speaker may say. McClendon (47) reported his findings on the relationship between note-taking and listening comprehension, while Brewster (7) conducted, among college freshmen, an exploratory study of some aspects of critical listening.

Another study of freshmen students, one concerned with the relationship between listening comprehension and two aspects of speech competency —vocal ability and communicative ability—was conducted by Stark (56). For additional studies about college students, the reader may refer to those conducted by Biggs (5) and Haberland (28; 27). The *Fifth Mental Measurements Yearbook,* edited by Buros,[1] provided two articles on the "Brown-Carlsen Listening Comprehension Test: Evaluation and Adjustment Series" (41; 43). There are also two articles on "Sequential Tests of Educational Process: Listening" (42; 44).

Two studies were concerned with evaluation—Brown's (9) and Irvin's (34). Brown (9) attempted to establish, if possible, a relationship between listening and academic success. Among other things he found that:

1. Students in three different surveys rated listening more important than reading as a factor in achieving academic success.

2. Listening ability was about as closely related to semester marks as was reading ability.

3. For students graduating "with high distinction" and "with distinction" from the University of Minnesota, the average percentile rank in reading of those graduating with high distinction was 78, and in listening it was 92. For those graduating with distinction the average percentile rank in reading was 78 and in listening 81.

4. There is a need for evaluating student performances in listening as well as in reading.

[1] Oscar K. Buros, editor. *Fifth Mental Measurements Yearbook.* Highland Park, New Jersey: Gryphon Press, 1959. p. 577-82.

Irvin (34), working with 2,400 freshmen, evaluated a program of listening training on the basis of (a) whether a program of listening training would improve listening skills, (b) whether a difference in listening skills existed between the sexes, and (c) whether the time of day during which students listened had any influence on their listening proficiency. Training proved helpful, men proved to be better listeners than women, and the time of day had little if any relevance.

In the elementary school. Concerned with primary children, Launderville (38) cited the results of her study, which indicated that listening tests can be used to measure the varying listening abilities of first graders and that they are as effective as reading readiness tests for predicting success. Hayes' (32) dissertation attempted to compare reading and listening comprehension of primary age children.

Summary

Interest in listening skills has continued to grow, and a certain amount of research has begun to accumulate. Data still are rather limited, however, and many studies are limited in scope such as those concerned with, for example, interrelationships between listening skill and reading ability. There are relatively few publications that offer direct, reasonably complete, and comprehensive advice to the teacher on ways of fostering listening skills.

Bibliography

1. BARBE, W. B., and R. M. MYERS. "Developing Listening Ability in Children." *Elementary English* 31:82-84; February 1954.
2. BECKER, SAMUEL L. "Research in the Teaching of English with Mass Media." *Elementary English* 38:398-403, 410; October 1961.
3. BECKER, SAMUEL L. "Teaching of English in the Mass Media." *Elementary English* 38:250-58; April 1961.
4. BEERY, ALTHEA. "Interrelationships Between Listening and Other Language Arts Areas." *Elementary English* 31:164-72; March 1954.
5. BIGGS, BERNICE P. "Construction, Validation, and Evaluation of a Diagnostic Test of Listening Effectiveness." *Speech Monographs* 23:9-13; March 1956.
6. BLACK, JOHN W. "Aural Reception of Sentences of Different Lengths." *Quarterly Journal of Speech* 47:51-53; February 1961.
7. BREWSTER, LAWRENCE W. "An Exploratory Study of Some Aspects of Critical Listening Among College Freshmen." *Speech Monographs* 24:86-87; June 1957.
8. BROWN, CHARLES T. "Studies in Listening Comprehension." *Speech Monographs* 26:288-94; November 1959.
9. BROWN, JAMES I. "Evaluating Student Performance in Listening." *Education* 75:316-21; January 1955.

10. Burns, Paul C. "Teaching Listening in Elementary Schools." *Elementary English* 38:11-14; January 1961.

11. Caffrey, John. "Auding Ability at the Secondary Level." *Education* 75:303-10; January 1955.

12. Caffrey, John. "Auding." *Review of Educational Research* 25:121-38; April 1955.

13. Canfield, G. Robert. "Approaches to Listening Improvement." *Elementary English* 35:525-28; December 1958.

14. Cartier, Francis A. "Listenability and 'Human Interest.'" *Speech Monographs* 22:53-57; March 1955.

15. Cashman, Paul H. "What Research Tells Us About the Development of Listening Skills." *Reading in Relation to Mass Media.* A Report of the Fourteenth Annual Conference and Course on Reading. Pittsburgh: University of Pittsburgh, 1958. p. 31-42.

16. Crosby, M. "Listening and Speaking for a Purpose." *Childhood Education* 36:255-58; February 1960.

17. Decker, Richard G. *Using Mass Media in Teaching English.* Albany, New York: Bureau of Secondary Curriculum Development, New York State Education Department, 1960. 61 p.

18. Dow, Clyde W. "Integrating the Teaching of Reading and Listening Comprehension." *Journal of Communication* 8:118-26; Autumn 1958.

19. Duker, Sam. "Goals of Teaching Listening Skills in the Elementary School." *Elementary English* 38:170-74; March 1961.

20. Duker, Sam. "Listening." *Review of Educational Research* 31:145-51; April 1961.

21. Edgar, Kenneth Frank. "The Validation of Four Methods of Improving Listening Ability." Unpublished doctoral thesis. Pittsburgh: University of Pittsburgh, 1961.

22. Forbes, A. E. "Listen Now." *Grade Teacher* 78:64-123; October 1960.

23. Fulton, Renee J. "Language Laboratories Develop the Listening Ear." *Modern Language Journal* 43:224-25; May 1959.

24. Furness, Edna L. "Proportion, Purpose, and Process in Listening." *Educational Administration and Supervision* 44:237-42; July 1958.

25. Furness, Edna L. "Remedial and Developmental Program in Listening." *Elementary English* 32:525-32; December 1955.

26. Goodman-Malamuth, Leo, II. "An Experimental Study of the Effects of Speaking Rate upon Listenability." *Speech Monographs* 24:89-90; June 1957.

27. Haberland, John A. "A Comparison of Listening Tests with Standardized Tests." *Journal of Educational Research* 52:299-302; April 1959.

28. Haberland, John A. "Speaker Effectiveness and the Brown-Carlsen Listening Test." *School and Society* 86:198-99; April 26, 1958.

29. Hampleman, R. S. "Comparison of Listening and Reading Comprehension Ability of Fourth and Sixth Grade Pupils." *Elementary English* 35:49-53; January 1958.

30. Harwood, Kenneth A. "Listenability and Rate of Presentation." *Speech Monographs* 22:57-59; March 1955.

31. Harwood, Kenneth A. "Listenability and Readability." *Speech Monographs* 22:49-53; March 1955.

32. Hays, Mary T. "Construction and Evaluation of Comparable Measures of English Language Comprehension in Reading and in Listening." *Dissertation Abstracts* 18:1721-22; No. 5; 1958.

33. HOSEY, GLADYS V. "Better Speech Through Better Listening." *Journal of Business Education* 34:172-73; January 1959.

34. IRVIN, C. E. "Evaluating a Training Program of Listening for College Freshmen." *School Review* 61:25-29; January 1953.

35. KEGLER, STANLEY B. "A Comparative Study of the Size and Nature of Reading and Listening Vocabularies." *Dissertation Abstracts* 19:2602; No. 10; 1959.

36. KELLEY, MARCELLA R. "Promoting the 'Listening' Habit in Kindergarten and Primary Grades." *American Childhood* 43:12-14; March 1958.

37. KING, W. H. "Experimental Investigation into the Relative Merits of Listening and Reading Comprehension for Boys and Girls of Primary School Age." *British Journal of Educational Psychology* 29:42-49; February 1959.

38. LAUNDERVILLE, MARY F. "A Study of the Effectiveness of a First Grade Listening Test as a Predictor of Reading Achievement." *Dissertation Abstracts* 19:3172; No. 12; 1959.

39. LEWIS, M. S. "Teaching Children To Listen." *Education* 80:455-59; April 1960.

40. LEWIS, T. R. "Listening." *Review of Educational Research* 28:89-95; April 1958.

41. LINDQUIST, E. F. "Brown-Carlsen Listening Comprehension Test: Evaluation and Adjustment Series." *Fifth Mental Measurements Yearbook*. Oscar K. Buros, editor. Highland Park, New Jersey: Gryphon Press, 1959. p. 577-78.

42. LINDQUIST, E. F. "Sequential Tests of Educational Progress: Listening." *Fifth Mental Measurements Yearbook*. Oscar K. Buros, editor. Highland Park, New Jersey: Gryphon Press, 1959. p. 578-79.

43. LORGE, IRVING. "Brown-Carlsen Listening Comprehension Test: Evaluation and Adjustment Series." *Fifth Mental Measurements Yearbook*. Oscar K. Buros, editor. Highland Park, New Jersey: Gryphon Press, 1959. p. 577-78.

44. LORGE, IRVING. "Sequential Tests of Educational Progress: Listening." *Fifth Mental Measurements Yearbook*. Oscar K. Buros, editor. Highland Park, New Jersey: Gryphon Press, 1959. p. 579-82.

45. MARKGRAF, BRUCE R. "A Survey of Listening Pedagogy in American Teacher-Training Institutions." *Dissertation Abstracts* 21:699-700; No. 3; 1960.

46. MARTEN, MILTON E. "The Relationship Between Expressed Interests and Listening Skills of Children in the Sixth Grade." Unpublished doctoral thesis. Bloomington: Indiana University, 1958.

47. McCLENDON, PAUL I. "An Experimental Study of the Relationship Between the Note-Taking Practices and Listening Comprehension of College Freshmen During Expository Lectures." *Speech Monographs* 24:95-96; June 1957.

48. MOYER, HAVERLY O. "Can Ear-Training Improve English Usage." *Elementary English* 33:216-19; April 1956.

49. NICHOLS, RALPH G. "Ten Components of Effective Listening." *Education* 75:292-302; January 1955.

50. NICHOLS, RALPH G., and PAUL H. CASHMAN. "The Approval Factor in Listening." *Education* 80:268-71; January 1960.

51. PRATT, EDWARD. "Experimental Evaluation of a Program for the Improvement of Listening." *Elementary School Journal* 56:315-20; March 1956.

52. SCHWARTZ, S. "What Is Listening?" *Elementary English* 38:221-24; April 1961.

53. SISTER M. K. HOLLOW. "Listening Comprehension at the Intermediate Grade Level." *Elementary School Journal* 56:158-61; December 1955.

54. SMITH, DORA V. "Learning To Listen, Listening To Learn in the Elementary School." *NEA Journal* 47:100-101; February 1958.

55. SNIDER, B. "Attitude of Kindergarten Children Toward Specially Prepared Story Materials." *Journal of Experimental Education* 28:207-18; March 1960.

56. STARK, JOEL. "An Investigation of the Relationship of the Vocal and Communicative Aspects of Speech Competency with Listening Comprehension." *Dissertation Abstracts* 17:696; No. 3; 1957.

57. STILL, DANA SWANK. "The Relationship Between Listening and High School Grades." Unpublished doctoral thesis. Pittsburgh: University of Pittsburgh, 1955.

58. TRIVETTE, SUE E. "The Effect of Training in Listening for Specific Purposes." *Journal of Educational Research* 54:276-77; March 1961.

59. WESTOVER, F. L. "Comparison of Listening and Reading as a Means of Testing." *Journal of Educational Research* 52:23-26; September 1958.

60. WITTY, PAUL A. "Some Results of Eight Yearly Studies of T.V." *School and Society* 86:207-209; June 21, 1958.

61. WITTY, PAUL A., and ROBERT A. SIZEMORE. "Studies in Listening." *Elementary English* 35:538-52; December 1958.

62. WITTY, PAUL A., and ROBERT A. SIZEMORE. "Studies in Listening—A Postscript. *Elementary English* 36:297-301; May 1959.

63. WITTY, PAUL A., and ROBERT A. SIZEMORE. "Studies in Listening: I. Relative Value of Oral and Visual Presentation." *Elementary English* 35:538-52; December 1958.

64. WITTY, PAUL A., and ROBERT A. SIZEMORE. "Studies in Listening: II. Relative Values of Oral and Visual Presentation, Lectures, Movies, Examinations, and Advertising Material." *Elementary English* 36:59-70; January 1959.

65. WITTY, PAUL A., and ROBERT A. SIZEMORE. "Studies in Listening: III. The Effectiveness of Visual and Auditory Presentations with Change in Age and Grade Level." *Elementary English* 41:130-40; February 1959.

Chapter Nine

Frère Jacques Is Out of Bed!

For many years the contacts that many American elementary school children had with a second language were limited largely to the rote learning of songs such as *Frère Jacques* and similar superficialities. In turn, secondary level pupils had similarly circumscribed experiences. Now Frère Jacques, as a symbol of foreign language, is not only wide awake—he is out of bed and moving ahead at a gallop!

While the teaching of foreign languages in elementary and secondary schools is not new, interest in instruction of this kind has become vastly more widespread in the United States since the early 1950s. During the past two decades, as improved communication and transportation have increased our opportunities for meeting and talking with people from all parts of the globe, there has been an increasing expression of need for instruction in foreign languages during the elementary years as well as in the secondary schools.

Vigorous but divergent opinions are expressed by sincere and dedicated people as to the reasons for teaching (or not teaching) a foreign language at all levels including the elementary school. Each proponent or opponent cites reasons why his viewpoint should be supported. In the following chapter some of the literature related to foreign language instruction will be reviewed to help the reader examine *his* viewpoints.

Teachers' concerns about foreign language instruction. Teachers are critically concerned about several questions which revolve around the problem of introducing a second language—particularly in the elementary school. Some queries from teachers whose views governed the selection of research to be scanned include the following:

1. Does knowledge of a second language contribute to one's understanding of other people and their culture?

2. What recent research data help in answering questions about how to begin foreign language instruction?

3. What are the advantages or disadvantages of beginning instruction in a foreign language at the primary or intermediate level?

4. What descriptions of current programs and practices in elementary schools are available?

5. Should the foreign language teacher be the regular classroom teacher or a special teacher?

6. What instructional tools are available and how can they be used to improve instruction in a second language?

Understanding Other Cultures

Certainly, no one would deny that all peoples of the world would profit from improved international relations. Reasoning from this premise, many people feel, as more and more Americans and other persons travel over the earth, that it is increasingly important for students in the United States to learn a second language. Several articles have been written to present the reasons why a second language is important.

Parker (81) feels that *all* Americans can and should learn to read and write a foreign language. He feels that knowledge of a foreign language, among other things, can contribute greatly to our understanding of foreign affairs. Miele (71) states that (a) Americans must be taught foreign languages in order to acquire a better understanding of foreign cultures; (b) American schools should teach more Russian, Chinese, Arabic, African, and Indian languages; and (c) "success" factors in the Armed Forces programs should be applied in universities and colleges by the establishment of Intensive Language Centers, if America is to continue as a respected leader in international affairs. Brickman (10) emphasized that existing facilities should be improved and programs in foreign language instruction should be established where none now exist.

Meyer (70) argued that language is important in understanding national cultures and proposed three simultaneous approaches to improved communication between the American people and foreign nations. Presenting a different point of view from most educators, Drummond (4) suggested that children learn a different language every year from third grade to the eighth grade. While they study each language, he proposes, they should simultaneously learn about the different countries, customs, and cultures. In the eighth grade, according to Drummond, each child would choose the language in which he intended to specialize.

The four writers cited here apparently hold that international understanding would be enhanced through greater numbers of bilingual Americans. Other writers, however, refute this claim by pointing to the antagonism that exists between certain European nations with many bilingual and multilingual citizens. They claim that friendship, cooperation, and mutual respect are not so much related to a person's *ability* to speak another language as they are related to his *attitudes*. Both points of view are mentioned to encourage the reader to reach his own conclusions.

Reviews of Research Pertinent to Foreign Language

Several writers have published articles which summarize research findings related to questions involving initiating, planning, implementing, and evaluating foreign language programs in elementary schools. These authors generally conclude that wide diversity in practice exists, that reliable research designs to assist in scientifically evaluating these programs are rare, and that more research is necessary before definite policies and practices can be advocated.

A summary of various studies and research in the field was completed as early as 1955 by Kaulfers (54). Reviewing, among others, the research of Penfield, Spaulding, Schenck, Halloran, and Manuel and the surveys of Mildenberger, Thomas, and Kaulfers, he reported as follows on the foreign language programs in elementary schools of eight to ten years ago:

1. Programs are usually initiated by parents, high school teachers, or elementary teachers.

2. Classes are frequently staffed by elementary teachers, with the aid of a refresher course or in-service training program.

3. Enrollments range from ten in an isolated school to 75,000 in Los Angeles.

4. The most common elementary level for initiating a program is fourth grade.

5. The average time allotment ranges from 15 minutes per day below grade three, to 20 minutes for grade three, to a half-hour in intermediate grades.

6. Most programs are voluntary.

7. Instruction below grade four is usually based on the aural-oral method; reading and writing are introduced gradually in upper elementary grades.

8. Radio and television language programs have been used successfully.

9. By 1954 almost all organizations of foreign language teachers had created a special section devoted to the nurture of foreign language in the elementary school.

In 1960 Carroll (15) pointed to the need for more research data on which to base foreign language programs. He presented certain findings that support or fail to support many current assumptions concerning foreign language; he also raised basic questions that demanded additional research. His findings included:

1. People differ greatly in the ease and facility with which they can learn foreign language. Results of studies suggest that the chances of learning a language to the point of practical usefulness are quite small for perhaps 10 to

15 percent of college students. At all levels, differences in language aptitude show considerable independence from differences in general intelligence.

2. With the exception of pronunciation, evidence suggests that children do not learn foreign languages better or faster than adults.

3. There is not sufficient evidence to conclude that the study of foreign language at the elementary level will result in "better" language students in high school.

4. Evidence suggests that language learning has transfer value for new language learning *providing* that the instruction was designed to provide for transfer.

5. There is need to amass statistics about expected rates of language learning and to get some idea of learning.

6. Our objectives for foreign language instruction need to be clarified.

7. There is a need to settle the question of the utility of the "language laboratory."

8. Teaching machines may have the effect of reducing individual differences in apparent foreign language aptitude.

Carroll (13) also surveyed research pertinent to "Foreign Language in the Elementary Schools" (FLES). As a result of this survey, he made the following conclusions:

1. There is some solid basis for the belief that young children can acquire good pronunciation more rapidly and easily than adults do under normal conditions.

2. Evidence appears to support the conclusion that *time* spent learning a foreign language is more crucial than *age* as such.

3. One can find reports of successful foreign language teaching at every grade level. Some researchers have recommended grades 3 or 4 as the best starting level.

4. It is probably a mistake to select children for foreign language on the basis of intelligence test scores or on the basis of reading skill. The best presently available method is a short trial period of language learning.

5. Evidence is lacking as to whether pupils who study foreign language in the elementary school have an advantage when studying language in high school and college.

6. There are no research reports of any adverse effect of FLES on progress in other school subjects.

7. There is no *one* method of teaching foreign language that should be emphasized. Foreign language instruction should always be introduced in its spoken form followed later by the written form.

In addition, after reviewing several studies pertinent to the topic, Johnston (48) provided some help as to the characteristics of a sound instructional program.

114

Foreign Language in the Elementary Schools

Earlier in this section it was stated that the improvement in the teaching of foreign languages did not gain real impetus until the 'fifties. While Cleveland's program had been in continuous operation since 1921 and while the Los Angeles program was introduced in 1943, it was actually 1953 when, with the encouragement of the United States Office of Education, the "Conference on the Role of Foreign Languages in American Schools" stimulated national interest. Since that time, programs have been introduced at a prodigious rate.

Cycle of interest and disinterest. Lehani (63) sets forth an interesting abridged history of foreign language study in the United States that indicates cycles of interest and indifference. His summary is as follows:

1935-37—A few modest articles were written and the question was raised, "Why study foreign languages?"

1937-39—Articles, slightly more numerous, indicated a rising interest in second languages.

1939-41—Articles advocating Foreign Languages in the Elementary School programs appeared. Army Specialized Training Program was set up.

1941-43—Interest greatly aroused, due to war, growth of support for children learning a second language. Public opinion in 1943 clearly indicated a desire "for more and better language instruction."

1943-45—Most active era for language teaching. International language proposed. Oral method in vogue. Interest declined after the war.

1945-47—Fair interest in modern languages but diminishing. Some persons advocated beginning language in grammar school.

1947-49—Abating interest and indifference. Answer affirmative that students wish to study languages.

1949-51—Still hard times for the languages. Few articles, if any, were in popular magazines.

1951-53—Foreign language on the march again. Government sanction occurred. Elementary experiments springing up in communities.

1953-54—Activity became feverish. Evidence gained from articles from last two decades suggests there is a language cycle of about ten years' duration.

A survey conducted by Mildenberger (75) revealed that at least 271,617 children from kindergarten through grade six were receiving foreign language instruction from their classroom teacher or a visiting teacher, as early as 1955. This was an increase of 62,000 pupils in one year. The greatest number studied Spanish (221,583); the second most popular language was French (46,849); and the third most popular was German (2,481). Reportedly 156,000 children were studying foreign language in Catholic elementary schools, with French (88,379) leading the list, followed by Polish (39,999), Italian (15,510), Lithuanian (7,991), Ukranian (1,984), Spanish (708), and Latin (105). Since he did not receive complete returns to his questionnaire and since the survey was not exhaustive, Mildenberger remarked that these figures are not absolutely accurate.

A questionnaire was sent by Frazier (30) to each of three different groups of fifty people—curriculum directors, elementary school supervisors, and college teachers of elementary education—to determine their concern about instruction in foreign language in the elementary school. College teachers made the poorest display of interest, and curriculum directors expressed the greatest concern for studying and improving language programs.

General discussion. Several articles by Mildenberger also provide us with pertinent information regarding FLES. In 1955 he (74) wrote an article which presented the history of the study of foreign language from Colonial times. Remarking about the growing demand for foreign language in the elementary schools, he mentioned the advent of "bootleg classes" which have existed in many schools—these being classes which were not explicitly approved by the superintendent or board of education.

After reviewing the status of FLES in 1957, Mildenberger (76) stated that the revitalized language movement in the elementary schools may well be the key to one of the major concerns of modern education—the successful teaching of international understanding. He also commented that the scientific validity of an early start in language learning had been indicated by the studies of two neurologists, Penfield and Roberts. Quoting from their work, Mildenberger wrote:

The optimum age for *beginning* the continuous learning of a second language seems to fall within the span of ages 4 through 8, with superior performance to be anticipated at ages 8, 9, and 10. In this early period, the brain seems to have the greatest plasticity and specialized capacity needed for acquiring speech.

Interesting conclusions as well as current trends in learning a foreign language were presented by Hildreth (44). Andersson (5) wrote that FLES programs broaden horizons and increase understandings of other persons and cultures. He concurs that young children learn oral language rapidly and accurately but advocates that foreign language instruction be correlated with other studies to retain interest and to increase fluency. While Eaton (24) is highly in favor of FLES, she says that high school study is not enough to assure that children will be facile in a second language. She also comments on some of the problems involved in establishing such a program: (a) the cost of an adequate program—a poorly financed program is worse than no program at all; (b) the need for capable teachers; and (c)

116

the coordination of foreign language instruction in the curriculum so that there is little lost in other subject fields.

In regard to this last point, it would seem that, if instruction in foreign language is important, then it deserves and should have a recognized and accepted place in the elementary school program. The point that some writers make in stating that there is no loss to other subjects since instruction in foreign language only requires 15 to 20 minutes each day seems doubtful. The question would still remain, "How would this time have been used if foreign language instruction had not been included in the school day?"

Patterns of conflict and consensus. Many knights in verbal armor have ridden forth to defend the glories or deplore the problems of teaching children in the elementary school a second language. Girard and Smith (35), as well as Adams and Bolton (1), engaged in debates on the values of foreign language instruction and provided some readable information for those interested in pros and cons. On the basis of a small sample of students, Robinson (86) stated, on the affirmative side, that foreign language instruction is not detrimental to the basic learning process. Joining the fray when reporting to the principals and teachers of Catholic schools in Ohio, Klenke (59) felt language instruction would not have to displace any other content area, since it could be combined with many fields. Suggestions for teaching procedures were also included in this article. Hoppock (46), when she criticized the effectiveness of foreign language instruction in the grades, almost immediately received a rebuttal from Eaton (24).

In general, those in favor of FLES instruction believe that through such a program (a) world understanding will be fostered; (b) the needs of communities with large numbers of foreign-born peoples will be better met; (c) young children will learn languages readily; (d) children are naturally interested in other languages; (e) American children will become better educated linguistically, just as are certain European children; and (f) the general population favors instruction in a second language at an early age. These statements are, of course, largely vigorous *opinions*.

The anti-FLES writer confronts his opponents with the following arguments: (a) the school day is already overcrowded; (b) pupil population is exploding—additional teachers and buildings are needed—and this means increased expenses with little money available for FLES; (c) many teachers are not adequately prepared to teach a second language; (d) learning a second language without any immediate need or opportunity to communicate in the language breeds artificial learning experiences; and finally, as was stated earlier, (e) many Europeans are multilingual but apparently neither friendliness nor understanding among their nations has been increased by multilingualism alone.

If you choose the affirmative side . . . Procedures for initiating a program in foreign language instruction have been outlined by Strouse (92), who recommended that the choice of the language to be taught should be made only after a consideration of the needs of the community. Her recommendations indicated (a) that the start of such a program should be on an experimental basis and that it should be carefully studied as it developed; and (b) that initial instruction should be in the third or fourth grade because of potentially close association with social studies. However, she felt no harmful effects need be anticipated if instruction were begun in the kindergarten. Included in the article were (a) certain basic criteria to be followed; (b) suggested methods for obtaining teachers; and (c) suggested teaching methods as well as the following admonitions to administration:

1. Study any existing programs
2. Consult with experts in the field of child development
3. Seek public support
4. Appoint committees to develop a program to suit the community
5. Set up the necessary budget
6. Establish centers for training teachers
7. Obtain qualified personnel
8. Plan a long-range curriculum
9. Provide means of evaluation.

Some suggestions for improving teaching. Helpful directions for the teaching of foreign language have been suggested by several writers. While some of these suggestions have been widely explored, they have not been universally adopted or scientifically evaluated. Recognizing that opinions as to the objectives to be obtained will be different, it is well to ask, in a given community: (a) Is the study of a foreign language incidental to the primary concern of having children learn about other cultures? (b) Is the study of a foreign language intended to lead to both skill in the language and an understanding of the culture? or (c) Is the study of foreign language to emphasize the ability to understand, speak, read, and write the language? The approaches to instruction in foreign language will vary with the goals sought.

Mildenberger (72) reviewed the "natural" (aural-oral) method of teaching a foreign language and described two types of foreign language programs which promised to be suitable in the grades. The first type emphasized the intensive but pleasurable learning of a new language with only listening comprehension and speaking ability emphasized for the first two years. Reading, until the child has an easy familiarity with the basic elements of the spoken language, was not introduced. As might be expected,

118

writing follows reading in this program. The teacher is assumed to be a specialist skilled in the spoken language and conversant with the everyday life of the foreign people. The second type, while more limited in attempting to achieve linguistic competence, offered better opportunity for the integration of foreign language instruction with the regular school program. This second type is an instructional program in foreign language that is directed by the classroom teacher. Mildenberger felt that the second type of program can function effectively. While not achieving the same degree of linguistic learning, this program introduces pupils to a second language and creates a readiness for more serious learning in later years. Reindrop (85) agreed with Mildenberger that pupils should not be confronted with written symbols until they feel comfortable in the oral use of language.

Guerra (38) commented that foreign language program advocates were enthusiastic but that many of their programs had never been properly evaluated. Guerra also said that one approach to a foreign language program is presently living up to its promise—the Foreign Language Children's Theater. He described how the theater provided opportunities for children to learn colloquial and idiomatic expressions and to review language forms and previously studied vocabularies. He contended that the children's theater not only achieved the linguistic objectives and the cultural values promised the public but that it also embraced a wholesome philosophy of education. In another article the same author (40) suggested that there comes a day when children are eager for more than oral language—reading will open a whole new area. He stated that not only speaking but reading and writing should be taught. Tyson (94) offered additional suggestions to teachers when he reviewed issues and questions related to programs developed in New Mexico.

Among aids to instruction in foreign language is a teacher's guide entitled "Beginning French Instruction in Grade Three," published by the Modern Language Association. A description of this guide appears in the article, "Foreign Language Instruction" (26), in the *French Review*. Johnston (49) listed the services that the United States Office of Education offers: (a) consultative services; (b) surveys and statistical studies; (c) teacher exchanges; (d) cooperative research; and (e) special programs.

When shall FL instruction be started? A comprehensive description of a foreign language program was written by Kaulfers (53) in 1956. Both he and DeSauze (18) stressed the necessity for continuity and articulation between language programs in the junior and senior high schools. In discussing the optimum age for beginning instruction in a foreign language, Larew (61) argued that his small sample of seven-year-olds attained satisfactory results. Boehm (7), also discussing age, reported on the 1959 proposal of the United States Office of Education that every child should study one foreign language from third through sixth grade. Through junior and senior high school, presumably, pupils should be permitted to take two languages. A different viewpoint was taken by Brickman (11) when he recommended that foreign language instruction should begin at the junior high school and also serve as a basis for senior high school history and social studies.

The Status of FL Practices

Although policies vary widely, many school systems throughout the country now offer programs of foreign language instruction in the elementary school. They commonly differ in (a) the language that is taught; (b) the age at which instruction is begun; (c) the person who directs instruction—classroom teacher, language specialist, or a combination of both; (d) the amount of time devoted daily to instruction; (e) the number of years that language instruction is offered; (f) the kind of children who may enroll in classes; and (g) the methods and materials employed by the teacher.

General descriptions of programs. Among descriptions of the teaching of French and Spanish are those written by Hoyt (47) about the schools of Fairfield, Connecticut, and by Geissenger (33) and McCormack (69) concerning the schools of Somerville, New Jersey. Both programs began instruction in the third grade. In the February 1956 issue of the *French Review* (27), the enrollment in foreign language programs in the New York City schools was discussed. Other writers who presented general accounts of programs were (a) Peacock (82), who treated summer school classes at Southern Illinois University; (b) MacRae (66), who dealt with practices in San Diego's elementary schools; and (c) Hartwig (42), who contributed a history of foreign language programs in the elementary schools of Carbondale, Illinois.

¿Habla usted español? Parlez-vous français? As indicated earlier, Spanish currently is the most widely taught foreign language. Suggestions for the teaching of Spanish in the elementary schools have been written by Foster and Williams (29), Etnire (25), Mattison (68), Larew (62), Spaulding (91), and Borst (9), all of whom provide information of a general and specific nature.

Ratte (83; 84), Mulhauser (78), Joyeaux (50), Grew (37), and Dunkel and Pillet (20; 21; 22) offered advice for those considering the introduction of French as a second language. Mulhauser's (78) article should be of particular interest to those who wish to compare the oldest language program—the Cleveland Plan—with more recently developed

FLES programs. Annual descriptions of the program at the University of Chicago as presented in the three articles by Dunkel and Pillet (20; 21; 22) merit serious consideration.

Helpful hints for instructional programs in German were given by Kirch (56), Kahn (52), Krauss (60), and Wittman (34). In addition to these reports, Letton and Henry (64) commented on teaching Russian; Castiglione (16) reported favorably on his experiment in the teaching of Italian; and Chomsky (17) discussed his recent experiences in the teaching of Hebrew in the United States.

Diversity in the choice of languages to be taught is supported by much general opinion which maintains that it made no difference what language is offered as long as skill in the second language is developed.

In the high schools. Elementary teachers who are interested in better articulation between the elementary and secondary grades may well care to read an article by Mildenberger (73). He described the national picture insofar as instruction in modern languages in the high schools is concerned. Some of the possible reasons for dropouts in high school language classes were itemized by Fulton (32). The relative value of certain variables in relation to success in foreign language study concerned Hascall (43).

In addition to these articles, Klee (58) discussed effective practices in secondary schools and offered teachers suggestions for making their modern language programs lively, active, and exciting. Justman and Nass (51), Skelton (90), and Carroll (14) were interested in achievement: (a) Justman and Nass (51) measured differences in achievement noted on the part of pupils who were or were not introduced to the study of foreign language in the elementary schools; (b) Skelton (90) compared high school students who had engaged in foreign language study and those who had not with respect to their freshman performance in college; and (c) Carroll (14) questioned whether the Modern Language Aptitude Test could predict the success of secondary school pupils in foreign language.

Who Shall Go Forth To Teach?

It was mentioned previously that one of the problems to be resolved— one of great concern to most educators—is by whom children should be taught a second language: (a) the classroom teacher, (b) a language specialist, or (c) a combination of the two. Unfortunately, there are not large numbers of qualified persons who can meet the criteria of knowledge of the language and knowledge of the learner, the learning process, and the teaching-learning situation.

Opinions are varied. Hill (45) reaffirmed a viewpoint with which many language instructors would agree, namely that language teachers have an important job to do and that they are devoted to doing it and presumably can do this job better than the classroom teacher whose foreign language skill is limited or rusty. In the *French Review* for May 1956 (28), the administrative staff of the Modern Language Association stated their opinion as to teacher preparation and certification—they believed that specific programs of preparation should be established by universities and that state certification should be required. This response is scarcely surprising!

Kirch (57) discussed the advantages or disadvantages of using specialists or regular classroom teachers in providing instruction for the elementary schools. He presented his conclusions as follows:

Advantages of Specialist:

1. Foreign language has been traditionally taught by specialists in the high schools and colleges.

2. They have better command of the language, better pronunciation, sentence rhythm, and accent.

3. Concentrating only on one subject, they have more time to perfect themselves and their methods of teaching.

4. They are more likely to attend foreign language teachers' association meetings and to read professional publications.

5. Many elementary teachers prefer to have specialists teach foreign language.

Disadvantages:

1. Instruction often can be given only for periods of 20 to 30 minutes on two to five days a week.

2. It is tedious when a special teacher has to repeat similar material so often.

3. Specialists are not always familiar with the elementary school curriculum, the elementary school as a whole, and the psychology of the young child.

Advantages of Regular Classroom Teacher:

1. They can best integrate the foreign language instruction into the regular school program.

2. They know the best methods for teaching young children.

3. The time for instruction and the length of instruction period can be more flexible.

4. Foreign language instruction is less open to attack from those who are not friendly when it is administered by regular classroom teachers.

Disadvantages:

1. There is not enough time to do an adequate job.

2. Teachers often are not fluent enough in the language.

3. They are less able to obtain suitable instructional materials.

122

Andersson (6) stresses the need for developing a partnership between elementary school teachers and language specialists. Recognizing that two points of view exist, he states that the important thing is that the teacher be both adequately prepared in foreign language and in the theory and practice of the elementary school. Clearly, in view of the limitations of *both* the specialist (who is more familiar with a second language than with the elementary school) and the classroom teacher (who may not know a foreign language well), it seems prudent to prepare more bilingual elementary teachers!

Can every teacher be an FL teacher? While making pertinent comments in regard to the interests of teachers of French, Harris (41) made definite recommendations directed toward building cooperation among French teachers at different grade levels. Guerra (39) suggested several techniques for future teachers of foreign language in the elementary schools, as did Adler (2) and Sister Ruth Adelaide (89). While stressing the value of foreign language study, Freeman (31) made the following points regarding the expansion of the teacher's horizons:

1. We speak of the need to broaden the *child's* view, but often forget that this requires *teachers* with wide interests and abilities.

2. There is a great need for Americans to learn to think in international terms.

3. There is no one foreign language uniquely better than any other for this purpose.

4. The study of a language in elementary school shows the child that a foreign language *can* be learned.

5. There is no way of predicting specific language needs in later life.

6. We must teach children that all thought is not housed in English.

7. We must help the child to see that different people think different, but still logical, thoughts.

8. We must break down the idea that Americans cannot learn a foreign language.

One solution to the question of having teachers not only knowledgeable about foreign language but knowledgeable about instructional practices for young children is to have more universities and colleges seriously engage in an adequate educational program for elementary foreign language teachers.

Educational Media and Foreign Language Instruction

Some individuals contend that educational media—films, filmstrips, tapes, phonographs, books, slides, auto-instructional programs and machines, as well as language laboratories—facilitate and vitalize the teaching and learning of foreign language. To such persons the use of newer media suggests possible solutions to problems that confront the schools as larger and larger numbers of students seek an education. Some believe that programed learning and language laboratories provide a good means for combining mass education with quality education; others believe that machines are too impersonal and constitute a threat to effective learning.

Friend or foe? Among persons concerned with the effects of the language laboratory on the development of skill in foreign language was Allen (3). He found that students who used the laboratory achieved significantly higher scores in reading, vocabulary, and grammar but that there was no difference in the degree of achievement in the oral performance of the groups studied. Mueller and Borglum (77) believed, as a result of their investigation, that students who attended laboratory sections profited from this experience and achieved more than students who did not attend.

Shane and Shane (87), on a subjective basis, stated that the expense involved in establishing language laboratories seems justified at high school and college levels. Two points these authors made should be considered: (a) more teachers will need to be trained in the use of the laboratory, and (b) more materials need to be developed for use in language laboratories.

A strong case for the use of language laboratories was made by Mathieu (67) and Desberg (19). King (55), in showing the importance of language laboratories, provided a frame of reference in regard to "teaching machines" and language laboratories. Bonin (8) described how laboratories could be used to open new techniques for teaching English to the foreign born.

Some of the disadvantages of language laboratories were cited by Trace (93) in 1959. In this same year, Mustard and Tudisco (79) published the results of a survey they began in 1957 in 253 foreign language departments in 57 colleges and universities in the United States. Their questionnaire, asking about specific undergraduate programs in French, German, Italian, Russian, and Spanish, was answered by 170 departments.

The uses of educational tools have been described by several writers. Glenn (36) reported on an experiment using radio lessons as a means of instruction in foreign language while the use of television was described by Nostrand (80) in the teaching of French, Lindstrom (65) in the teaching of Russian, and Buck (12) in the teaching of German. All three also agreed that television constituted an effective educational tool.

Summary

The teaching of a foreign language in the elementary school continues to receive much attention, with many persons strongly supporting the view that FLES is essential, while others say instruction should not begin at this level, and still others take a middle-of-the-road approach. Some of the questions which should be considered by a school contemplating introducing a second language were suggested in 1962 by Shane *et al.* (88:100ff.), whose comments also serve as a summary of FL problems and issues:

1. What are our purposes or goals in offering a program? Do we want our children to develop the ability to communicate in a foreign language? To develop a foundation for high school or college? To communicate with minority language groups in the area? Merely to learn a bit about a foreign tongue or culture rather than to speak and to understand it?

2. Does it seem likely that the learning of a second language can be made a functional experience for boys and girls in the local school situations?

3. What will we eliminate, decrease, or combine in the elementary school day to provide time for significant second-language experiences?

4. What is the probable long-range cost of second language instruction?

5. Can the school locate and employ able teachers of a second language who also are aware of the nature of the elementary school curriculum and who understand young children?

6. What language or languages shall be offered?

7. For which children shall experience with a second language be provided?

8. At what grade level do we wish to introduce children to a second language?

9. What methods shall be use in presenting a foreign language and what organization of instruction do these methods suggest or require?

10. How shall we evaluate the success of our efforts to teach a second language?

Bibliography

1. ADAMS, L. S., and F. E. BOLTON. "Foreign Languages in the Grades?" *NEA Journal* 45:444-45; October 1956.
2. ADLER, A. "Cultural Involvement Through the Teaching of Languages for Beginners." *Journal of Educational Sociology* 34:243-47; February 1961.
3. ALLEN, EDWARD D. "The Effects of the Language Laboratory on the Development of Skill in a Foreign Language." *Modern Language Journal* 44:355-58; December 1960.
4. "American Association of School Administrators' Convention Sounds a New Note." *Nation's Schools* 57:70; March 1956.
5. ANDERSSON, THEODORE. "The Teaching of a Second Language in the Elementary Schools: Issues and Implications." *Education* 75:490-97; 1955.
6. ANDERSSON, THEODORE. "The Teaching of Modern Languages in the Elementary School: A Language Teacher's View." *Education Outlook* 29; January 1955.
7. BOEHM, L. "Age and Foreign Language Training." *Modern Language Journal* 43:32-33; January 1959.

8. BONIN, A. I. "A Language Laboratory Approach to Teaching English to the Foreign Student." *Junior College Journal* 31:104-106; October 1960.

9. BORST, ROMA J. "A Survey of Needs and a Program for Parents, Teachers, and Pupils in Occasional and Part-Time Elementary School Spanish Classes." *Dissertation Abstracts* 16:2399; No. 12; 1956.

10. BRICKMAN, W. W. "Foreign Language Teaching." *School and Society* 81:150-55; May 14, 1955.

11. BRICKMAN, W. W. "Social Studies and Foreign Languages." *School and Society* 85:60; February 16, 1957.

12. BUCK, G. C. M. "German by TV." *Modern Language Journal* 43:391-92; December 1959.

13. CARROLL, JOHN B. "Foreign Languages for Children." *National Elementary Principal* 39:12-15; No. 9; May 1960.

14. CARROLL, JOHN B. "Use of Modern Language Aptitude Test in Secondary Schools." *Sixteenth Yearbook.* New York: National Council on Measurements Used in Education, 1959. p. 155-59.

15. CARROLL, JOHN B. "Wanted: A Research Basis for Educational Policy on Foreign Language Teaching." *Harvard Educational Review* 30:128-40; No. 2; Spring 1960.

16. CASTIGLIONE, P. B. "An Experiment: Teaching Italian at the Elementary School Level." *Italica* 33:13-15; March 1956.

17. CHOMSKY, WILLIAM. "Principles of Teaching a Foreign Language to Young Children: Experiences in Hebrew." *Modern Language Journal* 39:89-92; February 1955.

18. DeSAUZE, E. B. "Continuity and Articulation in the Study of Foreign Languages Between Elementary and Senior High School." *French Review* 28:536-37; May 1955.

19. DESBERG, D. "Automaticity: Language Learning Goal." *Educational Screen and Audio-Visual Guide* 40:172-74; April 1961.

20. DUNKEL, HAROLD B., and ROGER A. PILLET. "The French Program in the University of Chicago Elementary School." *Elementary School Journal* 57:17-27; 1956.

21. DUNKEL, HAROLD B., and ROGER A. PILLET. "A Second Year of French in Elementary School." *Elementary School Journal* 58:145-51; 1957.

22. DUNKEL, HAROLD B., and ROGER A. PILLET. "A Third Year of French in the Elementary School." Reprinted from: *Elementary School Journal.* Chicago: University of Chicago Press, 1959.

23. EATON, ESTER M. "Foreign Languages and the Librarian." *School Life* 42:12-13; January 1960.

24. EATON, ESTER M., and OTHERS. "Foreign Languages in the Elementary Schools— Yes!" *Modern Language Journal* 41:373-75; December 1957.

25. ETNIRE, ELIZABETH. "The Teaching of Spanish in the Second Grades." *Modern Language Journal* 39:15-16; January 1955.

26. FOREIGN LANGUAGE PROGRAM. *French Review* 29:253; January 1956.

27. FOREIGN LANGUAGE PROGRAM. *French Review* 29:336-38; February 1956.

28. FOREIGN LANGUAGE PROGRAM. "Teacher Preparation and Certification." *French Review* 30:494-95; May 1956.

29. FOSTER, D. P., and C. M. WILLIAMS. "Aural-Oral-Written vs. Aural-Oral in Teaching Spanish to Fourth Graders." *Modern Language Journal* 44:153-57; April 1960.

30. FRAZIER, A. "How Concerned Are We About Foreign Languages in the Elementary School?" *Educational Research Bulletin* 40:89-93; April 1961.

31. FREEMAN, S. A. "Expanding the Teacher's Horizons." *School and Society* 86:451-55; December 20, 1958.

32. FULTON, RENEE J. "The Problem of the Drop-Out in High School Language Classes." *Modern Language Journal* 42:115-19; March 1958.

33. GEISSINGER, J. B. "Foreign Language in Elementary Grades." *American School Board Journal* 133:27-29; August 1956.

34. WITTMAN, NORA E. "German in the Elementary Schools." *School and Society* 83:208; June 9, 1956.

35. GIRARD, D. P., and H. F. SMITH. "Foreign Language in the Elementary School?" *NEA Journal* 44:270-71; May 1955.

36. GLENN, LEONA. "Teaching Foreign Language by Radio." *Educational Research Bulletin* 40:113-20; May 1961.

37. GREW, JAMES H. "The Introduction of French in the Elementary Schools in Andover, Massachusetts: The Story of a Battle." *French Review* 28:419-24; April 1955.

38. GUERRA, MANUEL H. "The Foreign Language Children's Theatre: Methods and Techniques." *Hispania* 40:490-93; December 1957.

39. GUERRA, MANUEL H. "Future Teachers of Foreign Language in the Elementary School." *Modern Language Journal* 40:4-12; January 1948.

40. GUERRA, MANUEL H. "Is Conversation Enough? A Reappraisal of Beginning Foreign Language Instruction." *Hispania* 43:249-52; May 1960.

41. HARRIS, JULIAN. "An Editorial." *French Review* 31:64-66; October 1956.

42. HARTWIG, H. A., and A. A. FOLEY. "History of the Foreign Languages in the Elementary Schools Program in Carbondale, Illinois." *Modern Language Journal* 43:152-54; March 1959.

43. HASCALL, EDWARD ORSON. "Predicting Success in High School Foreign Language Study." *Dissertation Abstracts* 19:3245; No. 12; 1959.

44. HILDRETH, G. "Learning a Second Language in the Elementary Grades and High School." *Modern Language Journal* 43:136-42; March 1959.

45. HILL, ARCHIBALD A. "Language Analysis in Language Teaching." *Modern Language Journal* 40:335-45; October 1956.

46. HOPPOCK, ANNE S. "Foreign Language in the Elementary School—How Effective?" *Modern Language Journal* 41:269-71; October 1957.

47. HOYT, CARLYLE G. "Foreign Language in the Elementary Grades of Fairfield, Conn." *Education* 75:504-508; April 1955.

48. JOHNSTON, MARJORIE C. "Foreign Language Instruction." *Review of Educational Research* 31:188-96; April 1961.

49. JOHNSTON, MARJORIE C. "Foreign Language Teaching." *School Life* 41:16-18; September 1958.

50. JOYEAUX, G. J. "An Experiment in East Lansing." *Modern Language Journal* 41:144-45; March 1957.

51. JUSTMAN, JOSEPH, and MARTIN L. NASS. "The High School Achievement of Pupils Who Were and Were Not Introduced to a Foreign Language in Elementary School." *Modern Language Journal* 40:120-23; March 1956.

52. KAHN, LOTHAR. "Teaching German in the Elementary School: A Short Trial Course." *German Quarterly* 29:25-28; January 1956.

53. KAULFERS, WALTER V. "Earmarks of a Good Foreign Language Program." *California Journal of Secondary Education* 31:4-13; January 1956.

54. KAULFERS, WALTER V. "Foreign Languages." *Review of Educational Research* 25:154-65; April 1955.

55. KING, P. E. "Teaching Machines and the Language Laboratory." *American School Board Journal* 141:17-18, 35; August 1960.

56. KIRCH, MAX S. "At What Age Elementary School Language Teaching?" *Modern Language Journal* 40:399-400; November 1956.

57. KIRCH, MAX S. "Specialist or Classroom Teacher for Foreign Language in the Elementary School?" *Modern Language Journal* 42:132-35; March 1958.

58. KLEE, J. "Effective Practices in Secondary Foreign Language Teaching." *Modern Language Journal* 45:207-10; May 1961.

59. KLENKE, M. A. "Foreign Languages in Catholic Elementary Schools." *School and Society* 81:85-88; March 19, 1955.

60. KRAUSS, P. G. "Suggested Methods and Materials for Teaching German in Elementary Schools." *German Quarterly* 29:239-50; November 1956.

61. LAREW, LEONARD A. "Optimum Age for Beginning a Foreign Language." *Modern Language Journal* 45:203-206; May 1961.

62. LAREW, LEONARD A. "A Study of Spanish Articulation in the Elementary School: A Pilot Study." *Dissertations in Education.* Columbia: The University of Missouri Bulletin, Study 35, 1960. p. 114-17.

63. LEHANI, J. "Cycle of Interest and Indifference in Foreign Language." *Modern Language Journal* 39:355-60; November 1955.

64. LETTON, M. C., and N. B. HENRY. "Educational News and Editorial Comment: Teaching Russian in Grade III." *Elementary School Journal* 58:128-29; December 1957.

65. LINDSTROM, T. S. "Elementary Russian on Television." *Modern Language Journal* 43:389-90; December 1959.

66. MACRAE, MARGIT. "Teaching a Second Language in San Diego Elementary School." *Education* 75:509-12; April 1959.

67. MATHIEU, G. "Language Labs: Mechanical Monsters or Push-Button Miracles?" *California Teacher Association Journal* 56:8-10; September 1960.

68. MATTISON, HELEN. "A Fourth Grade Teacher of Spanish Reports." *Modern Language Journal* 40:259-60; May 1956.

69. McCORMACK, MARGARET C. "Buenos Dias or Bon Jour." *Education* 75:521-24; April 1955.

70. MEYER, A. E. "Language and Communication." *PMLA* 72:13-22; April 1957.

71. MIELE, ALFONSE RALPH. "Armed Forces Language Training in Peacetime (Since World War 2)." *Dissertation Abstracts* 19:135; No. 1; 1958.

72. MILDENBERGER, KENNETH. "Foreign Languages in the Grades." *American School Board Journal* 133:25-26; October 1956.

73. MILDENBERGER, KENNETH. "The National Picture of Modern Foreign Languages in the High School." *Modern Foreign Languages in the High School.* Marjorie C. Johnston, editor. U. S. Department of Health, Education, and Welfare, Office of Education, Bulletin No. 16, Part 2. Washington, D. C.: Superintendent of Documents, Government Printing Office, 1958. p. 41-49.

74. MILDENBERGER, KENNETH. "The Progress of FLES." *Education* 75:498-503; April 1955.

75. MILDENBERGER, KENNETH. "Status of Foreign Study in American Elementary Schools." Washington, D. C.: U. S. Department of Health, Education, and Welfare, Office of Education, Committee on Foreign Language Teaching, February 1956.

76. MILDENBERGER, KENNETH. "World Affairs, Languages and Children." *Scientific Monthly* 85:64-67; August 1957.

77. MUELLER, THEODORE, and GEORGE P. BORGLUM. "Language Laboratory and Target Language." *French Review* 29:322-31; February 1956.

78. MULHAUSER, RUTH. "Experiment or Tradition?" *Modern Language Journal* 40:462-64; December 1956.

79. MUSTARD, HELEN M., and ANTHONY TUDISCO. "The Foreign Language Laboratory in Colleges and Universities: A Partial Survey of Its Instructional Use." *Modern Language Journal* 43:332-40; November 1959.

80. NOSTRAND, H. L. "French by TV." *Modern Language Journal* 43:387-88; December 1959.

81. PARKER, WILLIAM R. *The National Interest and Foreign Languages.* Preliminary edition. U.S. State Department. Washington, D. C.: Superintendent of Documents, U. S. Government Printing Office, April 1954. 131 p.

82. PEACOCK, VERA. "Let's Teach Languages in the Grade School." *Illinois Education* 43:301; April 1955.

83. RATTE, ELIZABETH H. "Foreign Language for Some or for All." *Modern Language Journal* 41:355; November 1957.

84. RATTE, ELIZABETH H. "Lexington Elementary School French Class." *French Review* 28:444-47; April 1955.

85. REINDROP, REGINALD C. "The Reading Aim Re-Examined." *Modern Language Journal* 41:239-43; May 1957.

86. ROBINSON, H. R. "Educational News and Editorial Comment: Foreign Languages and Basic Learnings." *Elementary School Journal* 57:418-20; May 1957.

87. SHANE, M. L., and H. L. SHANE. "Laboratories for Foreign Language Teaching." *Educational Leadership* 18:293-98; February 1961.

88. SHANE, HAROLD GRAY; JUNE GRANT MULRY; MARGARET E. REDDIN; and MARGARET C. GILLESPIE. *Improving Language Arts Instruction in the Elementary Schools.* Columbus, Ohio: Charles E. Merrill Books, Inc., 1962. 526 p.

89. SISTER RUTH ADELAIDE. "The First Door to Foreign Language in the Elementary School." *Modern Language Journal* 42:172-74; April 1958.

90. SKELTON, ROBERT B. "High School Foreign Language Study and Freshman Performance." *School and Society* 85:203-205; June 8, 1957.

91. SPAULDING, SETH. "A Spanish Readability Formula." *Modern Language Journal* 40:433-41; December 1956.

92. STROUSE, ADELINE K. "The Place of Foreign Language Study in the Elementary Curriculum." *Education* 75:513-20; April 1955.

93. TRACE, A. S. "New Look in Foreign Language Instruction: Threat or Promise." *Modern Language Journal* 43:382-86; December 1959.

94. TYSON, I. M. "Foreign Languages and the Elementary School." *Educational Forum* 25:209-12; January 1961.

Chapter Ten

Masses of Media

WHEN language arts research conducted prior to 1955 was reviewed in the ASCD monograph, *Research Helps in Teaching the Language Arts,* no section of the publication was given over to educational media per se. This void can be explained in two ways.

First, the several hundred teachers who were polled in 1954 did not, for the most part, ask that writings and research pertaining to mass media be reviewed. Their 49 basic types of questions, derived from 1,300 separate queries, were concerned with reading ("Should I use word analysis procedures in grade one?"), spelling ("Is it necessary to use a basic word list?"), handwriting ("When should the changeover be made from manuscript to cursive writing?") and so on. Second, relatively little research related to mass media (insofar as such media had a *direct* bearing on the language arts) was widely circulated prior to the early 1950s.

Five to eight years later the situation had changed appreciably. Teachers by 1959 expressed a lively interest in knowing more about the role of mass media. The term "communication skills," too, had permeated their vocabularies. Also, educational writings related to mass media and communication had appreciably increased. The present chapter briefly samples research and opinion up to early 1962 that pertain to the "masses of media" with which our schools are becoming acquainted.

The Status of Mass Communication and Educational Media

Indicative of the growing but not-yet-sharply-focused interest in mass communication and educational media were numerous general questions from teachers. Their tenor was, "What is happening in the language arts with respect to new media?" and, "What do these developments imply for the classroom teacher?" Some answers to these scatter-gun inquiries made about mass communication and educational media may be found in "broad overview" publications of the past few years.

Broad overviews. An Indiana University bulletin and several articles are helpful means of acquainting the language arts teacher with recent trends in educational media. Bern and others (9) presented, in an 83-page review, developments in such realms as airborne television. In two articles, Klapper (31; 32) discussed respectively the impact of mass communication and the directions research was taking, while Stein (54) dealt with the newer media as an educational challenge.

A simple, explicit statement by Willey (58) reviewed the role of audio-visual methods in developing communication skills, and Miller (38) enumerated certain barriers to more graphic communication and identified what he believed to be needed research projects.

Other useful articles anent communication were written by Smith (53) and Strickland (55). While not directly concerned with educational media, their viewpoints regarding language and communication make rewarding reading and have relevance insofar as instructional methods are concerned. Nunnally (42) reported on research dealing with the use of motion picture film at the primary level, and Agree's (1) research bore on the library as a materials center. The *London Times Educational Supplement* (17) recently included a succinct résumé of educational programming broadcast by the British Broadcasting Corporation during 1961-62. The résumé should prove of value to those interested in mass media developments overseas.

Communications research in review. Summaries of research that are helpful to the student who seeks, on his own initiative, to delve into educational media were made by Kumata and Deutschmann (33) in the AERA's *Review of Educational Research*. The status of communications research was assayed by Schramm, Riesman, and Bauer (47). Of particular pertinence in this article is Riesman's comment that "Work in the field of communications is inviting at the moment because of its very ambiguity and lack of structure."

Berelson (8) also appraised the state of communications research and concluded that study in this realm, as distinct from study in the area of educational media, was in a state of decline by 1959. Foshay (21) reviewed research involving new educational media in a 1960 yearbook, while Gerbner (22) treated content analysis and critical research in mass communication.

The discerning reader quickly will recognize that "communication" and "educational media" publications are scrambled together in the preceding paragraphs. The articles mentioned, however, are few enough in number so that this grouping of publications should pose no serious problem to the reader.

Writings with a Psychosocial Focus

A modest number of the reports reviewed focused on the social and psychological impact and implications of mass communications and educational media. Peripherally, at least, these promise to be provocative to the language arts teacher.

Breed (13), writing in *Social Forces* a few years ago, produced a thoughtful analysis of the influence of mass media. Included were such points as their diverse purposes and their relation to power and to class structure. An interesting viewpoint also appeared in the *London Times Educational Supplement* (40) during 1961, the gist of the article being that mass media were fostering false or faulty concepts. British culture, the writer lamented, was being overlaid with American influences which resulted from the historical fact that the United States exported media (e.g., TV westerns) that reflected a "frontier mentality" redolent of aggressiveness and individualism.

Lorge (34) presented a psychologist's concept of communication in a helpful and authoritative article, and Albert (2) discussed the critic or reviewer of mass media products as a cultural mediator and a person who should be especially ethical and perspicacious because of his influence on the perceptions of the general public.

Other psychosocially slanted publications of more than passing merit include Noelle-Neumann's (41) commentary on mass media and public opinion and Winthrop's (59) study of the effect of personal qualities such as sex and campus popularity on one-way communication at the college level. The Winthrop sampling of 100 students suggested that a speaker's sex did not appreciably affect the agreement or disagreement of the listener, but that collegians did tend to agree with the views expressed by the more popular students and to reject the views of their unpopular peers.

Also worthy of note: Fahey's (19) discussion of the influence of mass media on children's experiences. Among his points:

1. Knowledge can be communicated to a child through mass media of communication but the real live model has much greater potential for reinforcing learning.

2. Mass media constitute a source of environmental stimulation for most children but their impact is greater on some than others due to differences in exposure time.

3. Sometimes, because of brevity of presentation and lack of consistent follow-up, much of what is communicated does not convert into action tendencies.

4. Often knowledge, attitudes, and values are not communicated effectively by mass media but mass media can reinforce tendencies already begun.

5. Mass media can provide rich opportunities for the communication of experiences and are influenced by what the audience will accept.

132

TV: A Cyclops [1] of Growing Power

Television, a mere eye-straining novelty in the 1940s, became an important factor in the average home in the United States during the early 'fifties. In the closing years of the past decade, this medium of mass communication also began to be an important element in education. The rapidly growing educational influence of TV in home and school is strongly reflected in the increasing quantity of research and general literature now in print. In short, the Cyclops-like machine that modified American family life and created a mutation in home building (plus endless shifting of furniture!) has grown up enough to go to school.

Data related to TV are, in the following pages, sorted out and presented in terms of (a) the impact of television; (b) the status of instructional or educational TV; (c) evaluations that have been made of its influence; and (d) a few hard-to-classify reports that simply are listed as miscellany.

The impact of television. An overview of the increasing impact of TV can be obtained by comparing a 1951 report by Maccoby (35) with the more recent of the annual reports made by Witty and others (60; 64; 62). Maccoby's interview study in Cambridge, Massachusetts, is of historical interest since it represents the data collected by early investigators (e.g., children spent four hours watching TV on Sundays in 1950-51).

While all of the Witty *et al.* studies are interesting, the "Tenth Yearly Study and Comments . . ." in *Elementary English* (62) is of special usefulness because of the comparisons made possible after a decade of record-keeping. Representative of Witty's findings:

1. In 1950 children watched TV, on the average, 21 hours per week. This was the average amount of televiewing a decade later.

2. Elementary pupils watched TV an average of 12.3 hours per week more than did high school students.

3. Over a period of years, favorite programs change and new programs become popular.

4. In 1950, 43 percent of the elementary students had TV as compared to 99 percent ten years later.

5. TV-related problems in adjustment and behavior continued to be reported by teachers and parents.

6. Over a period of 10 years, westerns as well as "crime and violence" programs remained favorite programs of children.

7. Study showed little relationship between the grades made by children and amount of time spent televiewing.

[1] Sometimes misused, *Cyclops* (sī'klops) is a singular noun. The plural form is *Cyclopes* (sī-klō'pēz). The Cyclopes were members of a mythical race of one-eyed Sicilian giants, one of whom proved a hazard to Ulysses and his men during their long homeward journey.

8. Recently children were reading somewhat more widely than before TV was available.

The influence of TV on academic achievement was studied by Greenstein (25), who learned that, in the Chicago area at least, televiewing had no notable bearing on grades earned by elementary school children—except that his non-TV group made better grades in penmanship. Scott (48) sampled 465 Californians in grades seven and eight and discovered that the heavily addicted televiewers did less well in mathematics and in reading than did their peers. Zucker (65), on the other hand, contended that TV could be used to motivate reading.

In Britain, Welson (56) found television had reduced cinema-going by 33 percent, and 21 percent of his survey participants replied that their interest in cinema attendance also had waned.

Instructional TV. The reader interested in the topic will find a growing freshet of publications in recent years pertaining to the educational use of TV. A 1962 *NEA Research Bulletin* (39), for instance, reported teachers' and principals' opinions as to whether television could improve the quality of education. A large plurality of respondents felt that "some" but not "considerable" improvement was possible. Explicitly, 51.1 percent of the elementary school teachers and 66.3 percent of the elementary school principals believed that, *if classes were maintained at the present size,* teaching by television held promise for at least *some* improvement in the quality of education. On the other hand, about twice as many teachers (29.2 percent) as principals (14.7 percent) thought that there was promise of *little if any improvement.*

A majority of the teachers, 81.6 percent, and a majority of the principals in districts having 50 or more teachers believed that, with teaching by television, classes cannot be increased in size without detrimental effects on quality of education.

Teachers' opinions were not borne out by research in St. Louis, Missouri, done by Herminghaus (26). His data indicated that pupils in large-group classes at the ninth grade level achieved at least as well as pupils in conventional classes utilized as control groups. Sherman (52) has indicated the importance of making of careful study of the possibilities of massive educational improvements through airborne television,[2] while Brish (15), in his research, found encouraging evidence that closed circuit television was working out well in science education—the field in which he made his inquiry.

Shansky and Wilson (50) reported favorably on the use of TV in the Milwaukee public schools, while an article by McGrath (36) favorably

[2] Airborne TV began its third year of innovation and experimentation in the Midwest early in 1963.

evaluated the outcomes of Pittsburgh's use of instructional TV since 1955. Perry (43) contributed a useful discussion of teaching by television. Bivens' (11) article in a 1960 *NASSP Bulletin* reviewed the widely publicized program begun some years ago at Hagerstown, Maryland. His observations included the following:

1. TV . . . reflects the content and beliefs considered important, useful, and appropriate in a school system.

2. Effective TV . . . depends upon the ability of the teachers and associative personnel to plan, organize, and follow through on learning situations that are worth while and serve as an incentive to pupil action.

3. TV must be coordinated with other experiences.

4. TV does not replace instructional aids, but opens up new areas for them.

5. TV benefits larger numbers of students.

6. TV utilizes resourceful people of community, state, and nation.

Writing in a popular journal, Reddy (45) warmly lauded instructional television as represented by the nationally telecast programs of "Continental Classroom." Among his interest-capturing statistics were these: by 1960, over 1,000,000 persons watched the program; 96 percent of a group of participants polled felt that the program was helpful; 1,333 professors and classrooms would have been needed to teach and to accommodate the persons enrolled at a given time in "Continental Classroom."

Other writings of interest pertaining to educational TV included Sherburne's (51) views on ETV research in the decade ahead and Hoban's (28) thoughtful comments. Quotes from his 1958 article follow:

. . . the facts to date established by ETV research do not indicate that ETV has produced a major educational breakthrough as the simple consequence of application of a new technology of communication in education (28:165).

Many of the articulate proponents of ETV have sought to raise our hopes for educational solutions on condition that we install and operate TV in education. In so doing, they have in effect reduced the complex process of education to an existing technology of electronic representation of picture and sound (28:169).

Plainly, the general concern with instructional television is increasing, and data and opinion in print are likely to increase rapidly in the mid-1960s.

Evaluation and appraisal of TV. Of special appeal to teachers is the matter of actual research which has suggested to what extent TV is proving effective as a classroom tool. Brandon (12) conducted an experiment to determine the relative effectiveness of lectures, interviews, and discussions. He found that:

1. Programs utilizing the interview and discussion methods of presentation are significantly more interesting than are programs utilizing the lecture method of presentation.

2. The three methods of presentation do not differ significantly in their ability to communicate information.

3. More information is learned during the second and third ten-minute segments of a half-hour television program than during the first ten-minute segment.

Jacobs and Bollenbacker (29), working with 315 Cincinnati sixth graders, compared TV and conventional instruction in science. The sample was stratified with three ability levels identified by pre-experiment tests. For the high level, the group receiving instruction by television scored significantly higher than the group who received instruction by regular classroom methods. For the low level, those in the regular classroom scored significantly higher than the television group. For the middle level, both methods seemed equally effective.

In yet another study in the Pittsburgh area, Himmler (27) appraised TV teaching in reading, arithmetic, and French. Twenty classroom groups of fifth grade children participated. Some of his findings are as follows:

1. There was little observable difference between the instructional effectiveness of the TV teaching program and regular classroom instruction.

2. The TV lessons excelled those of the regular classroom teacher in most phases of presentation, especially in the employment of visual and enrichment materials.

3. Pupil interest in TV lessons is likely to be high if there is a maximum use of enrichment materials, if there is variety in the lessons, if skills presentations are suitably paced, and if there is provision for a substantial amount of active pupil participation.

4. Reading was more suitable for TV than was either of the other subjects.

5. Teachers and principals felt that the supplementary teaching program was necessary for the success of TV teaching.

6. The program provided valuable direct and indirect in-service training for teachers.

7. Teachers are not likely to welcome TV except as a short-term experience.

8. Open circuit TV seems desirable so that parents might become acquainted with the program.

Barrow and Westley (4), with the cooperation of 233 sixth grade children in eight Wisconsin classrooms, concluded that TV instruction resulted in more learning than when subject matter was taught by radio; but after a six-week interval the difference was no longer statistically significant. Bingham (10) explained in 1960 why the Washington, D. C., schools dropped classroom TV (e.g., TV disrupted regular instructional programs; telecasts took too much time; the programs failed to coincide sufficiently with regular study plans). Also of relevance: Bridges' (14) notations on an elementary school attention scale for evaluating educational

TV and, at the university level, a report from a committee established by the American Association of University Professors (46) which formulated, as of 1961, proposed policies to govern ETV.

In 1960, Jacobs and Bollenbacker (30) published the results of a teacher-pupil opinion poll of instructional television. On the whole, both teachers and youngsters expressed positive or favorable attitudes which did not coincide with points made by Bingham (see preceding paragraph). Less academically able children especially liked TV.

Miscellaneous television studies and reports. Several "general interest" articles merit mention because, at least peripherally, they bear on the improvement or challenge of mass media in relation to language arts instruction. Albert and Meline (3) did research on the way in which the use of TV was influenced by social status. Sample finding: prohibiting a child to teleview as a disciplinary device or punishment is more common among the "lower social status" group than among the "upper level."

Greenhill (24) made suggestions for improving communication and research therein, and Gerrish (23) discussed TV in relation to the industrial arts.

Summary

Since communication skills and mass media are topics associated with or relevant to the language arts, a modest number of studies and articles were reviewed in preparing this monograph. It seems likely that educational writers are directing more of their attention to educational media—a point borne out by the fact that writings concerned with educational media are on the increase.

In comparison with such fields as reading and handwriting, research and writings germane to media such as TV are a bit conflicting and sometimes seem to be less formally designed. In the next decade this situation probably will change appreciably as the role of education media becomes more sharply delineated, more widely accepted, and better understood.

Bibliography

1. AGREE, ROSE H. "Building a Library Enrichment Program." *Elementary English* 37:159-63; March 1960.
2. ALBERT, ROBERT S. "The Role of the Critic in Mass Communications: I. A Theoretical Analysis." *Journal of Social Psychology* 48:265-74; November 1958.
3. ALBERT, ROBERT S., and HARRY G. MELINE. "The Influence of Social Status on the Use of Television." *Public Opinion Quarterly* 22:145-51; Summer 1958.
4. BARROW, LIONEL C., and BRUCE H. WESTLEY. "Comparative Teaching Effectiveness of Radio and Television." *Audio-Visual Communication Review* 7:193-208; Summer 1959.

5. BECKER, SAMUEL L. "Research in the Teaching of English with Mass Media." *Elementary English* 38:398-403, 410; October 1961.

6. BECKER, SAMUEL L. "Teaching of English in Mass Media." *Elementary English* 38:250-58; April 1961.

7. BELSON, WILLIAM A. "Selective Perception in Viewing a Television Broadcast." *Audio-Visual Communication Review* 6:23-32; Winter 1958.

8. BERELSON, BERNARD. "The State of Communication Research." *Public Opinion Quarterly* 23:1-6; Spring 1959.

9. BERN, H. A. "New Directions in Audio-Visual Communication." *Indiana University School of Education Bulletin* 36:1-83; November 1960.

10. BINGHAM, ANDREW W. "D. C. Schools Drop Classroom TV." *Journal of Teacher Education* 11:29-30; March 1960.

11. BIVENS, DOUGLAS M. "Educational By-Products of TV Teaching." *National Association of Secondary-School Principals Bulletin* 44:262-64; April 1960.

12. BRANDON, JAMES R. "An Experimental Television Study: The Relative Effectiveness of Presenting Factual Information by the Lecture, Interview, and Discussion Methods." *Speech Monographs* 23:272-83; November 1956.

13. BREED, WARREN. "Mass Communication and Socio-Cultural Integration." *Social Forces* 37:109-16; December 1958.

14. BRIDGES, C. C. "Attention Scale for Evaluating ETV Programs." *Journal of Educational Research* 54:149-52; December 1960.

15. BRISH, WILLIAM M. "Closed Circuit Television for Science U.S.A." *Communications Media and the School.* Yearbook of Education, 1960. George Z. F. Bereday and Joseph A. Lauwerys, editors. New York: World Book Company, 1960. p. 216-21.

16. DECKER, RICHARD G. *Using Mass Media in Teaching English.* Albany, New York: Bureau of Secondary Curriculum Development, New York State Education Department, 1960. 61 p.

17. "Developments in Broadcasting." *London Times Educational Supplement* 2399: 975; May 12, 1961.

18. EDLING, JACK V., editor. *The New Media in Education.* Sacramento: A Report of the Western Regional Conference on Educational Media Research, Sacramento State College, and the California State Department of Education in cooperation with the U. S. Department of Health, Education, and Welfare, Office of Education. Sacramento, California: the College, 1960. 99 p.

19. FAHEY, GEORGE L. "Psychological Implications of Current Mass Media on the Experiences of Children." *Reading in Relation to Mass Media.* A Report of the Fourteenth Annual Conference and Course on Reading. Pittsburgh: University of Pittsburgh, July 1958. p. 77-87.

20. FORD FOUNDATION and the FUND FOR THE ADVANCEMENT OF EDUCATION. *Teaching by Television.* New York: Ford Foundation, 1961. 87 p.

21. FOSHAY, ARTHUR W. "New Media—Research Findings in the U. S. A." *Communication Media and the School.* Yearbook of Education, 1960. George Z. F. Bereday and Joseph A. Lauwerys, editors. New York: World Book Company, 1960. p. 231-41.

22. GERBNER, GEORGE. "On Content Analysis and Critical Research in Mass Communication." *Audio-Visual Communication Review* 6:85-108; Spring 1958.

23. GERRISH, H. H. "Industrial Arts Electronics for Televiewing." *Industrial Arts and Vocational Education* 50:22-23; June 1961.

24. GREENHILL, L. P. "New Directions for Communications Research." *Audio-Visual Communication Review* 7:245-53; Fall 1959.

25. GREENSTEIN, JACK. "Effect of Television upon Elementary School Grades." *Journal of Educational Research* 48:161-76.

26. HERMINGHAUS, EARL G. "Large-Group Instruction by Television: An Experiment." *School Review* 65:119-33; June 1957.

27. HIMMLER, MERWIN L. "An Analysis and an Evaluation of a Television Demonstration of the Teaching of Fifth Grade Reading, Arithmetic, and French." *Dissertation Abstracts* 17:2467-68; No. 11; 1957.

28. HOBAN, CHARLES F. "Hope and Fulfillment in ETV Research." *Audio-Visual Communication Review* 6:165-71; Summer 1958.

29. JACOBS, JAMES N., and JOAN BOLLENBACKER. "An Experimental Study of the Effectiveness of Television vs. Classroom Instruction in Sixth Grade Science in the Cincinnati Public Schools, 1956-1957." *Journal of Educational Research* 52:5; January 1959.

30. JACOBS, JAMES N., and JOAN BOLLENBACKER. "Teacher and Pupil Opinions of Instructional Television." *National Association of Secondary-School Principals Bulletin* 44:71-78; March 1960.

31. KLAPPER, JOSEPH T. "What We Know About the Effects of Mass Communication: The Brink of Hope." *Public Opinion Quarterly* 21:453-74; Winter 1957-1958.

32. KLAPPER, JOSEPH T. "Whither Mass Communications Research." *Public Opinion Quarterly* 22:177-79; Summer 1958.

33. KUMATA, HIDEYA, and PAUL J. DEUTSCHMANN. "The Mass Media: Journalism, Broadcasting." *Review of Educational Research* 28:148-58; April 1958.

34. LORGE, IRVING. "How the Psychologist Views Communication." *Teachers College Record* 57:72-79; November 1955.

35. MACCOBY, ELEANOR E. "Television: Its Impact on School Children." *Public Opinion Quarterly* 15:421-44; Fall 1951.

36. McGRATH, J. "Pittsburgh Pupils Have Two Teachers per Classroom for TV Lessons." *Nation's Schools* 58:35-42; July 1956.

37. "Midwest Program on Air-Borne Television Instruction." *Clearing House* 35:318-20; January 1961.

38. MILLER, NEAL E., issue editor. "Graphic Communication and the Crisis in Education." *Audio-Visual Communication Review* 5:1-120; December 1957.

39. NATIONAL EDUCATION ASSOCIATION. "Teaching by Television." *NEA Research Bulletin* 40:7-8; February 1962.

40. "New Iconoclasm: Mass Media Attacked." *London Times Educational Supplement* 2398:904; May 5, 1961.

41. NOELLE-NEUMANN, ELISABETH. "Mass Communication Media and Public Opinion." *Journalism Quarterly* 36:401-409; Fall 1959.

42. NUNNALLY, NANCY. "Primary Films as a Factor in Promoting Conceptual and Factual Learning in Kindergarten Children." Unpublished doctoral thesis. Bloomington: School of Education, Indiana University, 1955.

43. PERRY, ARNOLD. "Teaching by Television in Today's Schools." *Educational Forum* 24:389-95; May 1960.

44. POSTMAN, NEIL, and ASSOCIATES. *Television and the Teaching of English.* New York: Appleton-Century-Crofts, Inc., 1961. 138 p.

45. REDDY, J. "They Go to School at Dawn: Continental Classroom." *Readers Digest* 76:75-78; January 1960.

46. "Report of Committee C: Policy on Educational Television." *American Association of University Professors Bulletin* 47:145; June 1961.

47. SCHRAMM, WILBUR; DAVID RIESMAN; and RAYMOND A. BAUER. "Comments on 'The State of Communication Research.'" *Public Opinion Quarterly* 23:6-17; Spring 1959.

48. SCOTT, LLOYD F. "Relationships Between Elementary School Children and Television." *Journal of Educational Research,* Vol. 52; No. 4; December 1958.

49. SHAFER, ROBERT E. "Mass Communication." *Review of Educational Research* 31:197-207; April 1961.

50. SHANSKY, A. T., and A. T. WILSON. "Television in Milwaukee Public Schools." *American Teacher Magazine* 45:11-12; December 1960.

51. SHERBURNE, E. G. "ETV Research in the Decade Ahead." *Audio-Visual Communication Review* 8:192-201; July-August 1960.

52. SHERMAN, M. "Toward Education by Airborne Television." *Indiana University School of Education Bulletin* 36:62-76; November 1960.

53. SMITH, DORA V. "Teaching Language as Communication." *English Journal* 49:167-72; March 1960.

54. STEIN, J. W. "Mass Media: An Educational Challenge." *Peabody Journal of Education* 38:161-66; November 1960.

55. STRICKLAND, RUTH G. "Creative Expression in Language." *Childhood Education* 34:8-11; September 1957.

56. WELSON, WILLIAM A. "The Effect of Television on Cinema Going." *Audio-Visual Communication Review* 6:131-39; Spring 1958.

57. WILLENS, ANITA J. "TV—Lick It or Join It?" *English Journal* 49:639-40; December 1960.

58. WILLEY, R. D. "Using Audio-Visual Methods in Teaching Communication." *Elementary English* 31:276-84; May 1954.

59. WINTHROP, HENRY. "Effect of Personal Qualities on One-Way Communication." *Psychological Reports* 2:323-24; September 1956.

60. WITTY, PAUL A. "Children and T.V.: A Sixth Report." *Elementary English* 32:469-76; November 1956.

61. WITTY, PAUL A. "Televiewing by Children and Youth." *Elementary English* 38:103-13; February 1961.

62. WITTY, PAUL A. "Tenth Yearly Study and Comments on a Decade of Televiewing." *Elementary English* 36:581-86; December 1959.

63. WITTY, PAUL A., and OTHERS. "Studies of Children's Interest—A Brief Summary, Part III." *Elementary English* 38:33-36; January 1961.

64. WITTY, PAUL A., and PAUL KINSELLA. "Children and TV—A Ninth Report." *Elementary English* 35:450-56; November 1958.

65. ZUCKER, M. J. "Television: A Spur to Reading." *Elementary English* 37:44-46; January 1960.

Chapter Eleven

Improving Oral Language

ALTHOUGH children come to school knowing how to speak, they need many additional opportunities to improve this skill and to learn to express their ideas clearly and succinctly. Today's teachers, recognizing the importance of oral language, evidently are trying to provide every possible opportunity for each child to develop this skill to the best of his ability. Instead of using a highly formal approach to oral expression, teachers emphasize language as an essential tool in communication and give it a recognized place in the elementary and secondary school curriculum.

Questions related to speaking: This chapter attempts to answer questions which are directed toward the following concerns of teachers:

1. In brief, are there new studies touching on the broad, general topic of the history of speech?

2. What surveys of research have been published?

3. Is there any new information pertaining to the language development of young children?

4. How can good oral language programs contribute to effective communication?

5. Can you make some general suggestions for classroom teachers?

6. Are there rating scales that can be used to determine speaking effectiveness?

From Grunts to Oratory

When, why, and how man first began to speak will probably never be answered definitely, though many interesting theories and speculations have been presented by several writers. Books as well as articles have been written about man's progress from the grunts and growls of the remote past to the more polished oratory of today.

Langer (45) wrote an interesting essay about the origins of speech touching upon such questions as: (a) What generations invented language?

(b) What development of animal communication has eventuated into human communication? (c) What pre-Adamite thought of assigning a particular little squeak to a particular object? and (d) How did other pre-Adamites agree to assign the same squeak to the same thing?

Moving from "pre-Adamites" to a more recent era, Baskerville (2) reviewed the performance of orators during the latter part of the nineteenth and early twentieth century and found that there was considerable dramatic as well as literary criticism of oratory during this period. Raw materials for the studies of American public address can be found in the texts of speeches delivered by men attempting to mold public thinking about the issues of the day, said Auer (1), who also stated that congressional debates provide the largest body of speech texts now available.

Surveys of Research

Some research surveys which are available are directed to speech teachers, while others are directed to the regular classroom teacher. Since both groups should profit from studying the two types of literature, both are discussed in this section.

The results of a symposium dealing with speech education were reported in 1961 in the *NEA Journal* (68). Based on the writings of nine persons who are familiar with speech instruction, the essentials of a good speech program were described in the article. Listening as a part of the speech program also was discussed. Peterson (53) analyzed the basic problems of research in human communication, while Dow (19; 20) provided summaries in 1958 and 1959, respectively, of thesis abstracts in the field of speech.

The regular classroom teacher would benefit from reading the articles briefly reviewed by Wittick (82; 83). The authors included in the 1959 article were Bertram (4); Birch (5); Furness (27; 36); Jones, D. (39); Jones, M. (40); Pronovost (54); Seal (62); Wagner (77); and Woods (84). In 1960 Wittick (83) supplemented this list to include Carey (7); Curry (12); Cypreansen *et al.* (13); Davis (14); Furness (28); Gott (29); Kratovil (42); Luse (47); Schwartz (61); Smith, D. (65); Smith, L. (66); Wepman (78); and Wetmore (79). Many excellent suggestions are offered for teaching; methods and materials of instruction are included; and guides to effective speaking and listening are reviewed.

Language Development and Young Children

The language of children long has been a fascinating topic to many researchers. On what kind of loom were their language and thought woven? Not only does this question interest researchers; the general public as well seems attracted, entertained, and delighted by the imaginative and colorful speech of moppets.

In an article concerned with factors affecting speech development, Smith (65) said that although most people take speech for granted, children must be taught to speak. He also discussed (a) preliminaries to speech; (b) preparation for speech; (c) the role of the environment; and (d) factors which interfere with speech development. Sampson (58) reported on the continuation of a study on speech development involving 25 boys and 25 girls of 18-30 months of age which began in 1956. At the time of this report the same children were interviewed as close to their fifth birthdays as possible to obtain further information regarding their speech development. As a result of this longitudinal study, she concluded:

1. Although all children had shown progress, the results appeared to indicate that this progress was related to paternal occupation and the child's own intelligence quotient.

2. A comparison of previous and present ratings showed a low positive correlation.

3. The boys tended to score higher in precision of language (vocabulary); the girls tended to score higher in fluency. However, the differences were small.

Several studies have been concerned with the interrelationships among language variables. Martin (50) attempted to ferret out some of the significant factors in the language development of first grade children and to discover some of the interrelationships among these factors. At the University of Minnesota, Templin (71) studied four aspects of language: articulation of speech sounds, sentence structure, speech sound discrimination, and vocabulary, as well as the interrelations among these.

Sociometry and its relationship to the language structure of young children was investigated by Rosenthal (57) as he studied 358 second grade children in the California schools. His findings included the points that:

1. There are significant differences in the oral language patterns of children of high and low sociometric groups.

2. I. Q. was not statistically significant between high and low sociometric standing.

3. There was little difference between the high and low sociometric groups in the number of words used.

4. Children with a high sociometric standing used more meaningful oral language.

5. The language patterns of the high sociometric group were more active.

6. The high sociometric group used a greater variety of words.

7. The ratio of verbs to adjectives was higher among those in the high sociometric group.

8. The low sociometric group used far more word mazes than the high sociometric group and used them more often.

Effective Communication

As was stated earlier, language is an important tool of thought for communicating ideas to other people. Indeed, good oral language programs can contribute much to increasing the child's ability to interchange ideas and to relate to people of all ages—especially if they help him understand some of the subtle nuances of communication.

Some influences in communication. A report was published in 1955 by Crowell, Katcher, and Miyamoto (11) in which they discussed the results of their efforts to explore the relationship between self-concepts of communicative skill and performance in group discussion. Diehl, White, and Burk (17), in turn, presented their findings on the relationship between the rate of speech and effective communication. Investigating rhetorical clarity, Nebergall (51) reaffirmed the importance of recognizing that communication is a two-way process involving both speakers and listeners.

A pair of investigators, Diehl and McDonald (16), undertook to answer two questions: (a) To what extent does the quality of a speaker's voice interfere with his ability to communicate information? and (b) To what extent does a speaker's voice quality affect an audience's rating of his voice? They conducted an investigation concerned with five voice quality types: hoarseness, harshness, breathiness, nasality, and a voice free from these characteristics. They found:

1. Simulated breathy and nasal voice quality appear to interfere with a speaker's ability to communicate information. In the case of nasality, the difference, although statistically significant, is only slight.

2. Neither simulated harsh nor hoarse voice quality appears to have any negative effect on the ability of a speaker to communicate information. A reconsideration of the extent to which representative clinical types are handicapped seems indicated.

3. Such a reconsideration, however, should be made in view of the evidence obtained from college students' ratings of the various simulated voice quality types. A voice free from hoarse, harsh, nasal, and breathy characteristics they rated very good; a hoarse voice poor; a harsh voice only average; and a nasal voice only average.

4. The relationship between an audience's judgment of the goodness of a voice and the ability of that voice to communicate information appears to warrant further study.

Coyne (10) concerned himself with an investigation of how prestige influenced communication analysis while Thomas and Ralph (74) studied the effect of audience proximity on persuasion.

Communication and attitude change. Attitudes and attitude changes have long interested many teachers and researchers. Hovland (35) points out that two types of research are usually used to study attitudes in communication: experimental and survey. He also states that oftentimes a discrepancy is shown between the results of these two types of research caused usually by (a) differences in research design; (b) differences in the approach to evaluation; and (c) situational differences. According to the author, the results of both kinds of research are useful, and no one approach to research represents the only way to obtain necessary facts.

An informative study whose major purpose was to investigate group-centered and leader-centered roles and their different effects upon the feelings and attitudes of group members was published by Wischmeier (81) in 1955. The study of the development of leadership in small, relatively unorganized, highly motivated groups was pursued by Shaw and Gilchrist (63) as they explored intragroup communication and leader choice. Other articles on attitude and attitude change which the reader may choose to read include (a) Thistlethwaite, DeHaan, and Kamenetzky's (72) report on the effects of "directive" and "non-directive" communication procedures; (b) a study of the effects of intracellular and intercellular speech structure by Gulley and Berlo (30); and (c) Cervin's (8) investigation of how a change in group attitudes from opposition to cooperation affects individuals of the group.

Some Suggestions for Teachers

Teachers, today as always, are concerned with good instructional methods and better techniques for communicating ideas, information, and skills to learners. In contrast to the child in the early part of the twentieth century, today's child lives in a world in which effective oral communication is more important than ever before. As many voices besides that of the school compete for the ears of the child, it behooves the teacher to examine the literature and become familiar with interesting and informative ways of presenting information so that stimulating learning situations are created.

General information. To improve the young child's speech, Thompson (75) suggested objectives and activities to help teachers make speech improvement in the classroom both pleasant and fun. In turn, Fass (23) presented commendable practices developed by instructors of in-service programs which he felt would be interesting to teachers who have non-English speaking children in their classrooms.

French (26) reviewed the way that speech is taught in the schools of Atlantic City and illustrated how speech can motivate, enrich, and strengthen training in the other areas of the language arts. The superiority of speech training in speech improvement over leaving it to chance or hoping that maturation will improve speech is stressed by Hinze (33) in an article written in 1960. Feeling that interesting books help hold children's attention longer and stimulate them to respond to characters and action, Carey's (7) article suggested that the use of children's literature is a good method in speech therapy.

Two other articles may be of interest to teachers. Clevenger (9) provided a synthesis of findings regarding stage fright. He found that teachers of speech are not in agreement as to what constitutes the presence of stage fright. However, it might be comforting for females to know that, according to the judges in this study, the occurrence of stage fright is more common in men than in women. Another area for study is the disintegration of speech under delayed feedback. Such a study was completed by Leith and Pranko (46), when they examined how speech was affected under three different conditions when subjects were suddenly confronted with an experimentally induced stress situation.

Environmental factors: Environmental influences—the importance of heredity, home, school, and all parts of the total environment—are recognized as affecting the teaching-learning situation. The problems of teaching correct speech habits in the schools concerned Irwin (37), who held that it is the school's duty to eliminate, insofar as possible, impedimenta to freely flowing and precise speech in our students. He felt that the speech patterns of children were those of their parents and associates, many of which patterns were developed before the child entered school. For some children, it follows that they must unlearn their present incorrect habits of speech and learn the correct speech pattern.

The relationship between the quality of the child's language usage and the quality and types of language used in the home also interested Noel (52). After studying 124 pupils from 107 families, she reported:

1. The quality of language the child in the elementary grades uses is determined to a very large degree by the language which he hears his parents use.

2. The occupation of the father does not materially affect the quality of language used by the child when the intelligence quotient factor is held constant.

3. The more frequently parents participate in situations requiring the use of oral expression the better will be the quality of the child's language usage.

4. By constant practice on certain types of usage, the teacher can help the child eliminate some of his errors in those usages.

5. The cooperation of the parents with the schools in seeing that their children hear and practice correct English in the home is essential if much improvement is to be made in the quality of language used by their children.

Dawson (15) studied the vocabulary size of third grade pupils in relation to home-environment factors. After studying 131 third grade pupils

146

and 69 of the children's mothers from lower socioeconomic homes, she reported that the children's vocabulary size was comparatively low at the third grade level. Agreeing with the previously mentioned writers as to the importance of environmental factors, Dawson felt it possible that the educational attainment of the mother was a positive factor that contributed to the individual's language pattern. She also noted that, among these children, those with the more favorable home-environmental experiences had larger vocabularies and appeared to have greater possibilities for success in the language arts curriculum than those with meager home-environmental experiences.

Another study concerned with environmental factors was completed by Schlanger (59) as she undertook to assay the effect of institutional residence on the mental retardate's verbal output. Insofar as she was able to determine, children living with their parents were superior in language development. The home children achieved a mean sentence length of 5.36 words compared to the institutionalized children's mean of 4.18 words. The 64.9 words per minute score obtained by the children living at home was 15 words more than the mean of 49.7 of the institutionalized children. Schlanger also included a presentation of what she considered the causes for the differences in favor of the children living in their own homes. Teachers who are working with mentally retarded children would probably like to review Johnson *et al.* (38), who reported on speech language development of such children while enrolled in training programs.

Interrelationships between oral and written language. A nationally recognized expert, Strickland (70), emphasized the importance of oral language in the teaching of reading in a paper read in Pittsburgh in 1958 at the 68th annual meeting of the Alexander Graham Bell Association for the Deaf, Inc. She further affirmed that environment and experience, not native intelligence, determined the quantity and quality of language that children bring to school. Harrell (32; 31) studied 320 children from four age levels—9, 11, 13, and 15 years—for the purpose of describing and comparing various aspects of school age children's written and oral language. The results of this study are reported in his doctoral dissertation (32) and abridged in a journal article (31).

The interrelationships among language variables of children in the first and second grades—motor ability, oral language, drawing, reading, writing, and spelling—were appraised by Winter (80). Attempting to evaluate the effect of a method of phonic training which included (a) auditory training and (b) association of speech sounds with alphabetical symbols upon speech-sound discrimination and written spelling, Zedler (85) studied 232 second grade pupils in five Texas towns. On the basis of the results obtained from this experiment, the conclusions were:

1. Written spelling performance changes significantly and favorably with this method of training in phonics.

2. Speech-sound discriminative ability increases significantly with the phonic training.

3. Written spelling ability and speech-sound discrimination are significantly related variables.

Articulation and language ability. According to Horn (34), opinion in the field of speech correction has been divided over the question of when school children with articulation problems should be started in therapy. Evidently some studies indicate that therapy should not begin in the early grades since some reports show that articulation problems tend to decrease with maturation up to the fourth grade. Others argue that this ignores the fact that an untreated speech defect can create educational and adjustment problems in early school life. This is reported with other findings as a result of Horn's investigation into the relationship between misspelling and misarticulation. A survey of the literature of growth and developmental factors in articulatory maturation which develops the idea of relationships between maturation and other variables such as (a) chronological age, (b) intelligence, (c) reading, (d) retarded physical development, (e) sex differences, (f) handedness, and (g) race was published by Everhart (22) in 1960.

Steer and Drexler (69) were interested in determining the effectiveness of certain variables, measured at the kindergarten level, in predicting the articulation ability of the same children five years later. Moving to a slightly older group of children, Schneiderman (60) reported the results of her study—the relationship between articulatory ability and language ability in children six and seven years of age.

Evaluation

Some teachers have asked about scales or standardized tests that might be available to evaluate more precisely various aspects of language development. Several authors have focused their attention on this question. Using 200 boys and girls in grades four, five, and six in Massachusetts, MacDonald (48) administered tests which he had constructed to measure unaided recall after hearing a story, unaided oral recall after silent reading of a story, general information recall from common experiences, and imaginative oral elaboration based on story completion and picture completion. Fine and Zimet (24) reported on their study directed toward a quantitative method of scaling communication and interaction process. A technique for measuring speech effectiveness in public speaking class was described in an article by Fotheringham (25). Likewise, Smith (67) presented the results of his efforts to develop a measuring instrument for standardizing the meaning of speech related concepts.

Of interest to teachers is the scale which Laase (44) discussed in an article published in 1958. He reports the results of the study made at the University of Nebraska between 1948-55 to construct, validate, and experiment with a scale for students to rate teachers of speech. An empirically derived rating scale for intercollege discussion sequence was described by Richards and Pence (55), while Brooks (6) provided further information about evaluative techniques by publishing his work concerned with the construction and testing of a forced choice scale for measuring achievement in speaking.

After carrying on an extensive search through the standard indices of the speech, psychology, and educational journals to determine which tests were available, Douglas (18) in 1958 wrote an article discussing standardized instruments of speech measurement and the whole question of evaluation. He reported that only a few published tests of speech abilities could be found that claimed validation based upon a sizeable group of subjects. Douglas was not discouraged by this finding, however. He felt that a trained observer is the only practical means to the satisfactory testing of speech skills and that the training of the observer is the single most important factor.

Summary

Recognizing the increasing importance of oral skill in communication, writers continue to emphasize and re-emphasize the essential role that it plays and must play in children's early education. However, there is relatively little research that has been done in the realm of speech and language development. Much still is to be learned, and the need for continued research should be emphasized.

Bibliography

1. AUER, J. JEFFREY. "American Public Address and American Studies: A Bibliography of Work in Progress 1955, 1956, 1957." *American Quarterly* 9:217-22; Summer 1957.
2. BASKERVILLE, BARNET. "The Dramatic Criticism of Oratory." *Quarterly Journal of Speech* 45:39-45; February 1959.
3. BECKER, SAMUEL L. "The Effect of Instructional Methods upon Achievement and Attitudes in Communication Skills." *Speech Monographs* 27:70-76; March 1960.
4. BERTRAM, JEAN DeSALES. "Creative Dramatics in the School." *Elementary English* 35:515-18; December 1958.
5. BIRCH, JACK W., and OTHERS. *Improving Children's Speech*. Cincinnati: Cincinnati School Publishing Company, 1958. 46 p.

6. BROOKS, KEITH. "The Construction and Testing of a Forced-Choice Scale for Measuring Speaking Achievement." *Speech Monographs* 24:65-73; March 1957.

7. CAREY, M. "Children's Literature and Creative Speech." *Elementary English* 36:543-48; December 1959.

8. CERVIN, VLADIMIR. "Experimental Investigation of Behavioural Effects of Change in Group Attitudes from Opposition to Co-Operation." *Canadian Journal of Psychology* 9:155-60; September 1955.

9. CLEVENGER, THEODORE. "A Synthesis of Experimental Research in Stage Fright." *Quarterly Journal of Speech* 45:134-45; April 1959.

10. COYNE, JOHN M. "Prestige Suggestion Influences in Communication Analysis." *Dissertation Abstracts* 16: 1955; No. 10; 1956.

11. CROWELL, LAURA; ALLEN KATCHER; and S. FRANK MIYAMOTO. "Self-Concepts of Communication Skill and Performance in Small Group Discussions." *Speech Monographs* 22:20-27; March 1955.

12. CURRY, HERBERT L. "Howz Yer Speechin?" *Elementary School Journal* 60:24-25; October 1959.

13. CYPREANSEN, LUCILLE, and OTHERS. *Speech Development, Improvement, and Correction.* New York: The Ronald Press Company, 1959. 354 p.

14. DAVIS, DAWN. "Let's Reach for Speech." *Education* 80:74-75; October 1959.

15. DAWSON, MARTHA EATON. "A Study of Vocabulary Size of Third Grade Pupils in Relation to Home-Environmental Factors." *Dissertation Abstracts* 17:1515; July 1957.

16. DIEHL, CHARLES F., and EUGENE T. McDONALD. "Effect of Voice Quality on Communication." *Journal of Speech and Hearing Disorders* 21:233-37; June 1956.

17. DIEHL, CHARLES F.; RICHARD C. WHITE; and KENNETH W. BURK. "Rate and Communication." *Speech Monographs* 26:229-32; August 1959.

18. DOUGLAS, JACK. "The Measurement of Speech in the Classroom." *Speech Teacher* 7:309-19; November 1958.

19. DOW, CLYDE W. "Abstracts of Theses in the Field of Speech, XIII." *Speech Monographs* 25:84-149; June 1958.

20. DOW, CLYDE W. "Abstracts of Theses in the Field of Speech, XIV." *Speech Monographs* 26:87-148; June 1959.

21. EARLY, MARGARET J. "Communication Arts." *Encyclopedia of Educational Research.* Edited by the American Educational Research Association. New York: The Macmillan Company, 1960. p. 306-12.

22. EVERHART, R. W. "Literature Survey of Growth and Developmental Factors in Articulatory Maturation." *Journal of Speech and Hearing Disabilities* 25:59-69; February 1960.

23. FASS, F. "Seeking English-Speaking." *High Points* 42:53; December 1960.

24. FINE, HAROLD J., and CARL N. ZIMET. "A Quantitative Method of Scaling Communication and Interaction Process." *Journal of Clinical Psychology* 12:268-71; July 1956.

25. FOTHERINGHAM, WALLACE C. "A Technique for Measuring Speech Effectiveness in Public Speaking Classes." *Speech Monographs* 23:31-37; March 1956.

26. FRENCH, R. E. "Potential of Speech in the English Program." *English Journal* 49:556-62; November 1960.

27. FURNESS, EDNA LUE. "Is Your Speech Showing?" *Clearing House* 33:489-91; April 1959.

28. FURNESS, EDNA LUE. "Parallels in Speaking and Writing." *Education* 80:264-67; January 1960.

29. GOTT, SYLVIA RULFF, and ROBERT MILISEN. "Functional Articulatory Disorders." *Education* 80:468-70; April 1960.

30. GULLEY, HALBERT E., and DAVID K. BERLO. "Effects of Intercellular and Intracellular Speech Structure on Attitude Change and Learning." *Speech Monographs* 23:288-97; November 1956.

31. HARRELL, LESTER E., JR. "Comparison of the Development of Oral and Written Language in School-Age Children." *Society for Research in Child Development.* Child Development Publication, No. 66. Lafayette, Indiana: Purdue University, 1957. 77 p.

32. HARRELL, LESTER E., JR. "An Inter-Comparison of the Quality and Rate of Development of Oral and Written Language in Children." *Dissertation Abstracts* 16:1103; No. 6; 1956. 204 p.

33. HINZE, H. K. "Speech Improvement: An Overview." *Elementary School Journal* 61:91-96; November 1960.

34. HORN, R. E. "Relationship Between Misspelling and Misarticulation." *Journal of Speech and Hearing Disabilities* 23:294-97; April 1958.

35. HOVLAND, CARL I. "Reconciling Conflicting Results Derived from Experimental and Survey Studies of Attitude Change." *American Psychologist* 14:8-17; January 1959.

36. "In the Listener's Ear." *School Life* 40:5; June 1958.

37. IRWIN, R. "Problem of Assimilation." *Quarterly Journal of Speech* 46:302-303; October 1960.

38. JOHNSON, G. O., and OTHERS. "Speech Language Development of a Group of Mentally Deficient Children Enrolled in Training Programs." *Exceptional Child* 27:72-77; October 1960.

39. JONES, DAISY M. "So You Have Something To Say!" *Elementary English* 36:248-52; April 1959.

40. JONES, MORRIS VAL. "Choral Speaking in the Elementary School." *Elementary English* 35:535-37; December 1958.

41. KNOWER, FRANKLIN H. "Speech." *Encyclopedia of Educational Research.* Edited by the American Educational Research Association. New York: The Macmillan Company, 1960. p. 1330-32.

42. KRATOVIL, IRMA F. "The Voices of Children." *Education* 80:460-62; April 1960.

43. KRETSINGER, ELWOOD A., and NORTON B. YOUNG. "The Use of Fast Limiting To Improve the Intelligibility of Speech in Noise." *Speech Monographs* 27:63-69; March 1960.

44. LAASE, LEROY. "The Measurement of Instruction in Speech." *Speech Teacher* 7:47-53; January 1958.

45. LANGER, SUSANNE K. "The Origins of Speech and Its Communicative Function." *Quarterly Journal of Speech* 46:121-34; April 1960.

46. LEITH, W. R., and N. H. PRONKO. "Speech Under Stress: A Study of Its Disintegration." *Speech Monographs* 24:285-91; November 1957.

47. LUSE, ELEANOR M. "The Child Who Is Slow To Speak." *Elementary School Journal* 60:26-31; October 1959.

48. MACDONALD, DOUGLAS F. "The Construction and Evaluation of Objective Tests of Oral Language Skills." *Dissertation Abstracts* 17:1961-62; No. 9; 1957.

49. MALLORY, EDITH B., and VIRGINIA R. MILLER. "A Possible Basis for the Association of Voice Characteristics and Personality Traits." *Speech Monographs* 25:255-60; November 1958.

50. MARTIN, CLYDE. "Developmental Interrelationships Among Language Variables in Children of the First Grade." *Elementary English* 32:167-71; March 1955.

51. NEBERGALL, ROGER E. "An Experimental Investigation of Rhetorical Clarity." *Speech Monographs* 25:243-54; November 1958.
52. NOEL, DORIS I. "A Comparative Study of the Relationship Between the Quality of the Child's Language Usage and the Quality and Types of Language Used in the Home." *Journal of Educational Research* 47:161-67; 1953.
53. PETERSON, GORDON E. "Speech and Hearing Research." *Journal of Speech and Hearing Research* 1:3-11; March 1958.
54. PRONOVOST, WILBERT L., and LOUISE KINGMAN. *The Teaching of Speaking and Listening in the Elementary School.* New York: Longmans, Green and Company, 1959. 338 p.
55. RICHARDS, GALE, and ORVILLE PENCE. "An Empirically-Derived Rating Scale for Inter-Collegiate Discussion Sequences." *Journal of Communication* 6:69-76; 1956.
56. ROACH, BRUCE. *Speech Education in Texas Secondary Schools.* Research Study No. 25. Austin: The Texas Study of Secondary Education, April 1958. 28 p.
57. ROSENTHAL, R. "Some Relationships Between Sociometric Position and Language Structure of Young Children." *Journal of Educational Research* 48:483-97; December 1957.
58. SAMPSON, OLIVE S. "Speech and Language Development of 5-Year-Old Children." *British Journal of Educational Psychology* 29:217-22; November 1959.
59. SCHLANGER, BERNARD B. "Environmental Influences on the Verbal Output of Mentally Retarded Children." *Journal of Speech and Hearing Disorders* 19:339-43; September 1954.
60. SCHNEIDERMAN, NORMA. "A Study of the Relationship Between Articulatory Ability and Language Ability." *Journal of Speech and Hearing Disorders* 20:359-64; 1955.
61. SCHWARTZ, SHEILA. "New Methods in Creative Dramatics." *Elementary English* 36:484-87; November 1959.
62. SEAL, F. L. "Just How Trippingly on the Tongue?" *California Teachers Association Journal* 55:20-21; March 1959.
63. SHAW, MARION E., and J. C. GILCHRIST. "Intra-Group Communication and Leader Choice." *Journal of Social Psychology* 43:133-38; February 1956.
64. SHOOK, ANDREW W. "Auditory Sensitivity and Speech Defects—A Comparative Study of the Incidence of Selected Factors of Auditory Sensitivity and Defects of Voice and Articulation." *Dissertation Abstracts* 17:918; No. 4; 1957. 165 p.
65. SMITH, DAVID W. "Factors Affecting Speech Development." *Education* 80:452, 454; April 1960.
66. SMITH, LORETTA WAGNER. "Demonstration Classes in Speech Improvement." *Speech Teacher* 9:65-67; January 1960.
67. SMITH, RAYMOND G. "Development of a Semantic Differential for Use with Speech Related Concepts." *Speech Monographs* 26:263-72; November 1959.
68. "Speech Education: Symposium." *NEA Journal* 49:21-36; November 1960.
69. STEER, M. D., and H. G. DREXLER. "Predicting Later Articulation Ability from Kindergarten Tests." *Journal of Speech and Hearing Disorders* 25:391-97; November 1960.
70. STRICKLAND, RUTH G. "Interrelationships Between Language and Reading." *Volta Review* 60:334-36; September 1958.
71. TEMPLIN, MILDRED C. *Certain Language Skills in Children: Their Development and Interrelationships.* Monograph No. 26. Minneapolis: University of Minnesota Press, 1957. 183 p.

72. THISTLETHWAITE, DONALD L.; HENRY DeHAAN; and JOSEPH KAMENETZKY. "The Effects of 'Directive and Non-Directive' Communication Procedures on Attitudes." *Journal of Abnormal and Social Psychology* 51:107-13; July 1955.

73. THOMAS, GORDON L. "Effect of Oral Style on Intelligibilty of Speech." *Speech Monographs* 23:46-54; March 1956.

74. THOMAS, GORDON L., and DAVID C. RALPH. "A Study of the Effect of Audience Proximity on Persuasion." *Speech Monographs* 26:300-307; November 1959.

75. THOMPSON, B. K. "Improving the Young Child's Speech." *NEA Journal* 48:13-14; December 1959.

76. UTTERBACK, WILLIAM E., and WALLACE C. FOTHERINGHAM. "Experimental Studies of Motivated Group Discussion." *Speech Monographs* 25:268-77; November 1958.

77. WAGNER, GUY. "What Schools Are Doing in Correcting Language Disabilities." *Education* 79:450-52; March 1959.

78. WEPMAN, JOSEPH M. "Auditory Discrimination, Speech, and Reading." *Elementary School Journal* 60:325-33; March 1960.

79. WETMORE, THOMAS H. "The English Language." *Elementary English* 37:192-93; March 1960.

80. WINTER, CLOTILDA. "Inter-Relationships Among Language Variables in Children of the First and Second Grades." *Elementary English* 34:108-13; February 1957.

81. WISCHMEIER, R. R. "Group-Centered and Leader-Centered Leadership: An Experimental Study." *Speech Monographs* 22:43-48; March 1955.

82. WITTICK, MILDRED L. "Selected References on Elementary School Instruction; Speaking." *Elementary School Journal* 60:105-106; November 1959.

83. WITTICK, MILDRED L. "Selected References on Elementary School Instruction; Speaking." *Elementary School Journal* 61:107-108; November 1960.

84. WOODS, MARGARET S. "Creative Dramatics." *NEA Journal* 48:52-53; May 1959.

85. ZEDLER, E. Y. "Effect of Phonic Training on Speech Sound Discrimination and Spelling Performance." *Journal of Speech and Hearing Disorders* 21:245-50; June 1956.

DATE DUE		